The
NEEDLEPOINT
CROSS STITCH
book

The
NEEDLEPOINT
&
CROSS STITCH
book

Amelia Saint George
30 new charted patterns to create
your own designs

Photographs by Marie-Louise Avery

CONRANOCTOPUS

To Abigail and Tiphaine for their help,
effort and support. To Mummy and to Nana, who, at 85,
gallantly took up needlepoint to help out with backgrounds.
To absent Thomas, never say never.

Project Editor Patsy North
Art Editor Alison Fenton
Design assistant Alison Barclay
Production Julia Golding
Illustrators Paul Bryant, Elly King

First published in 1992 by
Conran Octopus Limited
37 Shelton Street
London WC2H 9HN

British Library Cataloguing-in-Publication Data
A catalogue record for this book is available from
the British Library

ISBN 1 85029 382 1

Typeset by Servis Filmsetting Ltd, Manchester

Printed in China

Acknowledgments and Suppliers

The author and publisher would like to thank the following for
supplying materials for photography:
For tapestry wools, pearl and stranded cottons, canvas, linens and
many needlework accessories:
DMC Creative World Ltd, 62 Pullman Road, Wigston, Leicester
LE8 2DY.
DMC Mercerie Service Relation Clientèle, 13 rue de Pfastatt, 68057
Mulhouse cedex, France.
For furnishing fabrics:
Bernard Thorp, 53 Chelsea Manor Street, London SW3 5RZ.
Bernard Thorp, 8 Avenue de Villers, 75007 Paris, France.
For their selection of luxurious braids, tassels and cords:
Turnell and Gigon Ltd, Chelsea Harbour, Lots Road, London
SW10 0XE.
Les Passementeries de l'Ile de France, 11 rue Trousseau, 75011
Paris, France.
For the chair on page 42 on which the butterflies flutter:
William L. Maclean Ltd, Wenstrom House, Brighton BN1 8AF.

The author also thanks the following for their contributions:
Richard Ginori, Milan, for beautiful porcelain; VV Rouleaux,
Fulham Road, London, for their exceptional selection of ribbons;
Peter Reed, Lomeshaye, Lancashire, for their exquisite sheets;
Dartington Jams, Ivybridge, Devon, for their delicious bottled
fruits and preserves; The Scotch House, Knightsbridge, London,
for the wonderful woollen travelling rug; Global Village, 247–249
Fulham Road, London SW3 6HY, for their sumptuous accessories.
For their advice and help, the author thanks:
Barrie Tolhurst, 25 Stable Way, Latimer Road, London W10.
Tel: 081 960 4503, for his help with all the upholstery.
Barbara Gundy, 59 Ebury Street, London SW1. Tel: 071 730 6407,
for her advice on all the framing.

Suppliers of embroidery materials
For details of stockists and mail order sources of the yarns and
fabrics used in this book, please contact the following addresses:
DMC Creative World Ltd, 62 Pullman Road, Wigston, Leicester
LE8 2DY. Tel: 0533 811040.
DMC Needlecraft Pty, 99–101 Lakemba Street, PO Box 131,
Belmore 2192, N.S.W., Australia. Tel: 010 612 5993088.

Courses
For further information on Amelia Saint George's courses in
designing for needlepoint and cross stitch, please write to:
12 Thurloe Place, London SW7 2RZ. Tel: 071 584 3863.

Contents

*i*ntroduction

Designing and making something oneself is a great joy, as I discovered when I picked up my pencil at the age of 30 and my needle shortly afterwards to begin my first venture into needlepoint and cross stitch design. I have not looked back since.

One of my early projects was the Butterfly and Fruit Chair illustrated on page 42. This chair is very special and a constant source of delight to me. It is like an old friend because of all the memories it evokes – the hours of pleasure I had while stitching it and the different conversations which it has stimulated. People frequently approach me if I am working on a piece of embroidery while travelling by train or plane and all these chance encounters and snippets of conversation have enriched my life.

One notable example was when I was flying to Chicago recently. The air hostess stopped to admire my work and remarked, 'Joe would just adore this.' In mid-flight Joe came and introduced himself. 'I'm the captain', he said. Noticing me glance nervously out of the window, he reassured me and got down to the subject that really interested him – needlepoint. He explained that it helped him to relax and that, when he was living out of a suitcase, it was his constant companion.

In the embroidery and design classes I now run, the first question I ask my students is 'Can anyone here draw?' Maybe one in twelve will admit to doing some sketching; the rest assume that they cannot. This is not, simply not, true. All my students eventually design their own work, admittedly some with more help than others and, if drawing skills are genuinely lacking, there are many sources of ideas which can be traced instead. I wrote this book to introduce the idea of creating one's own needlepoint and cross stitch designs rather than necessarily following a set of instructions word for word. In the chapters which follow I give you a wide range of versatile motifs to play around with and, to stimulate your natural creativity, I show you different ways of using the same basic images. These include fruit, roses, ribbons and bows, animals, alphabets, plaids, leaves and berries. You can then go on to create many more variations of your own.

For the complete beginner there are clear easy-to-follow charted patterns accompanied by instructions for stitching and making up the projects. Each motif is used in a simple way to begin with, then developed into repeating, cluster or scatter designs to show the wonderful selection of ideas which can arise from just one image. For more experienced readers, the designs can then be taken a stage further by arranging motifs into unique compositions. Within the book there are 30 separate designs, but in reality they can be developed to give an infinite number of possibilities.

For the home I like the idea of creating a fully coordinated interior with upholstery, cushions and tablecloths all showing variations on a theme and toning with one's own furnishings. This can easily be achieved by using the same motif, for example a rose, in needlepoint for a chair seat and also in cross stitch for a small decorative cloth. Clothes and accessories, too, can be given a personal touch with a cross stitch motif such as a bow or an initial and I demonstrate an impressively simple technique for working cross stitch on to fabric such as satin or velvet on which the threads cannot be counted.

My motto for those of you who are new to designing in needlepoint and cross stitch is: '*It's easy, you can do it.*' This book contains all the answers to my original questions and to those of my students, including information about materials, equipment, planning a design, making up cushions and simple upholstery. It will iron out any problems you might have, so that you can design and stitch with confidence.

materials & techniques

Whenever I have any spare time, I always enjoy picking up one of my current embroidery projects and working on it for a while. One of the great advantages of needlepoint and cross stitch is that you do not need a lot of different materials and complicated equipment – just evenweave fabric or canvas, needle and yarn, and a frame if you like using one. In this chapter I describe some of the fabrics and beautiful yarns available to the embroiderer and outline the basic techniques that will ensure successful stitching and give a professional-looking finish.

Stranded cotton, crisp white evenweave fabric and a few trimmings are all the materials required to make this trio of charming bibs.

Canvas

Needlepoint canvas is available in various widths and gauges, the gauge referring to the number of holes to 2.5cm (1in) in the canvas weave. It can range from a coarse rug canvas to a very fine petit point canvas. The larger-gauge canvas, having fewer holes to 2.5cm (1in), is quick to work up and produces a bulky item with a bold design, whereas a small-gauge canvas allows for more detail but is not as hard-wearing.

The main types of canvas are single thread and double (or Penelope) canvas. The single thread mono canvas has one weft and one warp thread crossing each other, while double thread canvas has two weft and two warp threads. The advantage of double canvas is that you can use petit point over single threads in some areas if you wish, while filling in other areas with tent stitch over the double threads.

Interlocking canvas is a type of single thread canvas in which the weft and warp threads are twisted together where they cross. If you are worried about your canvas deforming, this is the one to use. The single thread mono canvas is not twisted like this and will pull out of shape more easily if your tension is too tight. However, it is softer to hold and I prefer to use this type, especially for smaller projects.

When you buy canvas, allow at least an extra 5cm (2in) of spare canvas all round the area of your finished needlepoint to take stretching and turnings into account. For an upholstery project, add an extra 10cm (4in) of spare canvas all round.

Evenweave fabric

There are many different fabrics on the market for cross stitch work and your choice depends on your personal preference and the effect you want to achieve. The number of threads to 2.5cm (1in) is called the 'count' of the fabric. As with needlepoint canvas, a fine fabric with a high thread count such as 32 holes to 2.5cm (1in) will produce smaller stitches and therefore more detail than a coarser weave.

Evenweave linen is woven with single threads and comes in a variety of thread counts up to 36 per 2.5cm (1in). Hardanger fabric is woven with double weft and warp threads, while Aida is woven in blocks of threads, making it easy to count the holes. A child or beginner will therefore find Aida a good fabric to work with.

Yarns

Woollen and cotton embroidery yarns are produced in a dazzling array of colours. Four-ply tapestry wool can be used for a wide range of needlepoint projects. For finer work two-ply crewel wool is also suitable. I have used pearl cotton in two of the needle-point projects in this book, as this gives a beautiful sheen to the work.

For cross stitch, stranded cotton is ideal as the six strands can be separated and re-combined to make up the thickness you require. This also prevents the thread from tangling and gives a smoother finish. You can combine strands of different shades if you want to graduate the colour.

Stranded cotton

Pearl cotton

Tapestry wool

RIGHT
*W*oollen yarns produce a smooth, hard-wearing finish in needlepoint while embroidery cottons add a silky quality to your work. With crewel wool and stranded cotton, different coloured strands of the yarn can be mixed to give subtle shading.

OPPOSITE
*C*anvas and evenweave fabrics are available in a variety of gauges, widths and colours to suit every kind of needlepoint or cross stitch project.

Crewel wool

Whichever type of yarn you use, it should slip easily through the holes in the weave of the canvas or fabric, yet cover the surface well. Below is a guide to which yarns achieve the best coverage on various gauges of single canvas or fabric.

For 8-gauge to 14-gauge canvas, use 1 strand of tapestry wool.
For 16-gauge to 18-gauge canvas, use 2 strands of crewel wool or 1 strand of pearl cotton No.5.
For 8-count to 11-count Aida or Hardanger fabric, use 3 strands of stranded cotton.
For 14-count to 18-count Aida, use 2 strands of stranded cotton.

If you are designing your own project, one way to work out how much yarn you might need is to stitch a square inch (or 6.25 square centimetres) in the stitch and with the materials you are planning to use. On the basis of this, you can then estimate how much yarn will cover larger areas.

A useful guide for needlepoint is that an 8m (8.8yd) skein of tapestry wool covers an area of approximately 65 sq cm (10 sq in) in half cross stitch. Continental tent stitch would take double this amount.

Frames

Many people advocate using a frame for needlepoint and cross stitch. I personally prefer not to use one. When doing needlepoint I firstly always roll my canvas, never folding it as this deforms it. Secondly, when working on the middle section of a canvas, I roll each end towards the centre and pin the roll to secure it. I then work on the middle part, rather like on an ancient scroll. By pinning my canvas in this way, the 'scrolls' become a natural frame. This method has the added advantage that the part you are not working on remains clean, as it is rolled away out of sight.

Thirdly, and perhaps most importantly, is keeping an even tension, whether you are doing needlepoint or cross stitch. Just pull the thread gently until it lightly covers the canvas or fabric, and the embroidery is less likely to be stretched out of shape, whichever stitch you are using. However, for those who prefer to use a frame, there are many sizes of circular hoops and rectangular frames available for all types of project. When using a ring frame, remember to remove it from your embroidery at the end of each stitching session, so that it does not deform the evenweave fabric.

ABOVE

*C*hoose a yarn which gives good fabric coverage.

RIGHT
I prefer to work without a frame for needlepoint, just rolling my canvas.

Needles

Use tapestry needles for both needlepoint and cross stitch. These have a rounded tip which will not split the fabric threads. The only exception is for waste canvas, when you might need a pointed needle to go through the base fabric.

Tapestry needles range in size from 13 to 26, the higher numbers denoting the finer needles. Choose a needle size that will pass easily through the holes in your canvas or fabric without deforming them. As an example, a size 18 needle is suitable for 8-gauge to 10-gauge canvas, a size 20 needle for 12-gauge to 14-gauge canvas and a size 22 needle for 16-gauge to 18-gauge canvas.

Other materials

Do invest in some good embroidery scissors with sharp points for cutting threads. I attach a long ribbon to mine as they easily slip unnoticed amongst the skeins of thread. Use different scissors for cutting canvas or paper, as these will blunt your embroidery scissors.

As you can imagine, my finger has received the odd puncture from doing so much embroidery. However, I find thimbles difficult to cope with so I occasionally improvise with a fabric plaster.

A thread organizer is useful, especially if you are using a lot of colours. It is easy to make one yourself. Just punch some holes along the edge of a piece of card and loop the skeins through, writing the yarn numbers next to them. Thread organizers help when the light changes, as ·you can compare the yarn number written on the card to the number on the chart colour key.

Tracing paper is helpful when you are working out designs and selecting motifs to put together. Other materials you might need for planning and measuring out designs are a tape measure, pins, indelible marking pens (for canvas), tailor's chalk (for fabric) and water-erasable marking pens.

Lighting

When doing close work or matching colours, I strongly recommend using a daylight simulation bulb which has a blue finish. These can be obtained from any good art or health shop, and are inexpensive and kind to the eyes. A halogen lamp is equally good for colour matching, but is more expensive and demanding on the eyes.

Using the charts

The designs in this book are all given in the form of charts on which one square represents one tent stitch or half cross stitch (for needlepoint) or one cross stitch. The yarn numbers are given in a key, listed from dark to light.

As one of my aims is to encourage readers to work out their own designs, I have often used the same chart in various ways for different projects to show its versatility. You will therefore sometimes need to substitute different yarns and colours for the ones listed in the key. Or you can, of course, use your own choice of colours and enjoy creating a unique piece of embroidery.

*b*oth the blue and the green bows on the cloth can be worked from the chart (below). Simply substitute green yarns for the blue yarns in the same order of dark to light.

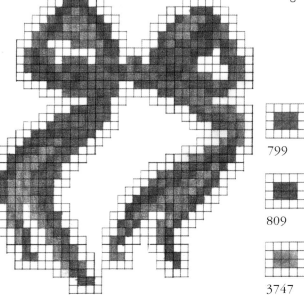

799

809

3747

Continental tent stitch

*t*he design on this cushion combines two of my favourite motifs – ribbons and butterflies. You can easily plan your own composition by linking motifs from various charts in the book. Remember that the charts can be used for both needlepoint and cross stitch designs.

Depending on the way each design is planned, you can either work from the chart exactly as it is shown, or you may need to isolate certain areas of it or re-arrange various elements within it. You may also need to combine motifs from one chart with those from a different chart. This will be explained more fully in the Planning & Designing chapter which follows.

Stitches

I have used cross stitch for the counted thread embroidery projects in this book, and tent stitch or half cross stitch for the needle-point projects. Half cross stitch uses only about half as much yarn as tent stitch, but is not as hard-wearing. Tent stitch is better for upholstery or anything that will receive a lot of wear. It can be worked in two ways: continental tent stitch and basketweave stitch. Basketweave stitch is ideal for back-grounds or large areas of the same colour as it distorts the canvas less.

1. This stitch is worked in horizontal rows from right to left and vice versa. Take diagonal stitches over one canvas thread intersection as shown.

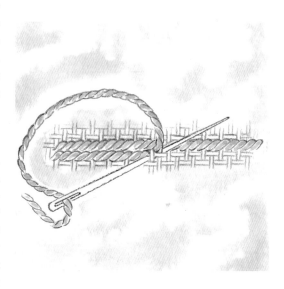

2. Work the second row from left to right. The stitches on the back of the work slope more than the stitches on the front.

Basketweave stitch

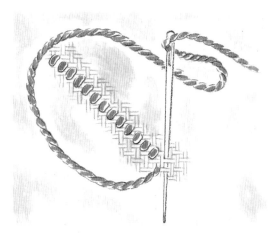

1. This form of tent stitch is worked in diagonal rows. For the first row, make a diagonal stitch, passing the needle vertically downwards for the next stitch.

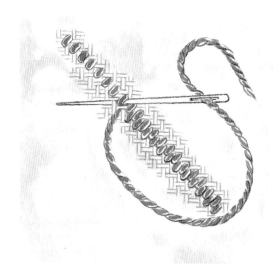
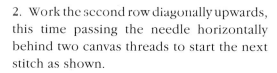

2. Work the second row diagonally upwards, this time passing the needle horizontally behind two canvas threads to start the next stitch as shown.

Half cross stitch

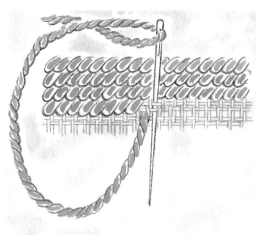

This stitch looks like tent stitch, but is worked differently. The stitches at the front of the needlepoint are diagonal, but those on the back are vertical.

Cross stitch

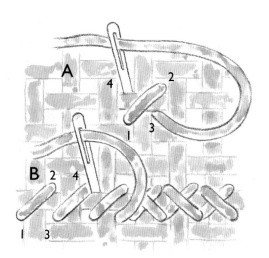

Each cross can be completed as you go along (fig. A). Or work the first row from left to right, then complete the crosses from right to left (fig. B).

1. Tack the waste canvas to the background fabric and work the cross stitch through both layers. I prefer to use evenweave fabric, although special waste canvas is available.

2. When the embroidery is complete, begin cutting away the excess waste canvas from around the stitched motif.

3. Continue cutting away the waste canvas, but leave thread ends long enough to pull out.

Preparing to stitch

To prevent the canvas from fraying while you are working on it, bind masking tape around the edges. With evenweave fabric, turn under or oversew the edges to stop them fraying.

When you start stitching, hold the end of the thread at the back of the fabric or canvas and catch it under the first few stitches to secure it. Never use a knot as this could work loose or form a lump under the work. To finish off, take the thread to the back of the embroidery and pull it through a few of the previous stitches.

I am often asked how long a thread I work with. I would recommend not more than 46cm (18in) for tapestry wool, stranded cotton and pearl cotton. With longer strands the wool begins to fray and the cottons to snag and untwist. Try not to carry yarn too far from one area to another underneath your work. These bridging threads are more vulnerable to wear, so try to make them no longer than 2.5cm (1in). With a framed picture such as a sampler, bridging threads will show through to the front of the work, so you will need to finish off each letter and number separately, however temptingly close they are on the chart.

Keeping fabric clean

It is sometimes a problem keeping lengths of fabric clean when working on a large project such as a tablecloth, a curtain, a sheet or a duvet cover. In this case, I roll up the part I have finished stitching and the part I have not yet reached and secure them inside dry-cleaning bags. With each end protected, I can then stitch the middle section, unrolling more fabric as I need it.

Using waste canvas

With this simple method, you can work a cross stitch design on to any fabric from organza to velvet, even though the threads of the fabric cannot be counted. The traditional

4. Pull out each individual thread of waste canvas from behind the cross stitch. The embroidered motif will be left neatly stitched on the background fabric. This method is ideal for woollen fabric, denim, fine cotton, satin or any fabric on which the threads cannot be counted easily.

material for the 'waste' canvas, which I prefer to use, is ordinary evenweave fabric. Tack a piece with a suitable thread count on to your chosen fabric over the area you wish to embroider. Then work the cross stitch as normal, through both layers of fabric together. You may require a needle with a sharp point in order to penetrate the bottom layer of fabric.

When the embroidery is finished, gently ease out the fabric thread by thread from behind the cross stitches, leaving the design on the base fabric. This method greatly appeals to my young daughters, and there is now a butterfly fluttering across a stain on a child's pale pink dress.

There is also a special 'waste' canvas available in different gauges for this technique. To remove this, you have to dampen the canvas to soften it and then pull out the threads one by one.

Stretching canvas

If your canvas has become deformed by the time you have finished it, you can stretch it back into shape. Cover a board with clean blotting paper, dampen the needlepoint to soften the canvas and place it face down on to the paper. Then, using rustless drawing pins or tacks, pin the needlepoint to the board around the edge of the canvas border. Work along each side from the centre outwards, stretching the needlepoint back into shape as you go. When it is completely dry, remove it from the board.

Pressing cross stitch embroidery

Cover the ironing board with a thick white towel. Place the embroidered article face down over the towel. Cover with a clean white cloth and press carefully with a warm iron. The thickness of the towel will prevent the stitches from being flattened.

planning & designing

Although you can follow any of the projects in this book using the same materials as I have done, one of my intentions throughout is to inspire you to create your own designs by combining the motifs in different ways to suit your individual requirements. You can take your pick of the motifs from each chapter, decide whether you want to work them in cross stitch or needlepoint, choose your own yarns and colours, and plan your own composition as you wish. In this way you can coordinate cushions, chair covers, table linen and many other items with your own home furnishings, at the same time expressing your individuality through your creative designing.

*i*t is easy to coordinate needlepoint and cross stitch designs with your home furnishings by planning your own colour schemes and arrangement of motifs.

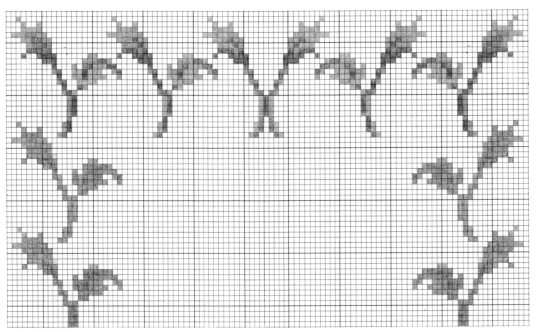

r oses and buds are very adaptable motifs. They can form a beautiful spray of flowers on a cushion (top) or be scattered at random over a fresh-looking tablecloth (above).

Arranging the motifs

The charted motifs in the book can be arranged in any number of different ways to create an original composition. Flower motifs are a good example of how this can be done. The rose-buds on page 52 or the thistles on page 121 can be used singly or as a scattered pattern. They can be arranged as mirror images or upturned. They can also be repeated in rows or reversed alternately, as in many traditional friezes.

When I use a motif as a mirror image, I just look at the charted design and reverse it in my mind. I soon get used to following a chart in this way – it is rather like driving on the opposite side of the road in a foreign country. Some of my students prop up a mirror on one side of the chart and follow the image in the mirror to help them become accustomed to working in reverse.

Flowers can overlap to vary a design, adding depth and interest to the composition. Bunches of flowers are always charming and you can create a new image by combining them with another motif from the

r ose-buds make effective borders. One side of this charted frame is a mirror image of the other with the rose-buds meeting and reversing at top centre.

book, such as a ribbon or a butterfly. For a really abundant feeling, why not compose an elaborate bouquet, using all the flowers, buds and leaves from the Roses & Buds chapter on page 46 and finishing off with a lavish bow and trailing ribbons?

Flower stems are very effective when overlapped and create interest when flowing out from a corner. On a border with a line of roses slanting in alternate directions, you can make a feature of crossing the stems. Remember, though, that when stems or ribbons cross or join one another, the eye is drawn to the cross or arrow formed, even if it is just a simple bud joining a main stem. Try to avoid too many arrows pointing into the centre of your work or having too many stems crossing, as a project will then look messy in spite of beautiful stitching.

Varying the background

With a cross stitch design, it is easy to vary the background by choosing a fabric with a slight pattern and working a design on to it over waste canvas. Certain patterns like checks and stripes can actually help you to place the stitches, like the fabric I used for the Frilled Cushion with Leaf Garland on page 102. On a plain evenweave fabric, a single cross stitch can be used to break up the background, as on the collar of the child's dress illustrated on page 58.

With needlepoint, any background is possible and you can add interest behind the main design by working a small scattered motif like a paisley. On the Wreath and Berries Cushion on page 106, I have achieved this by repeating the berry motif, while on the Red Bow Footstool on page 72, I have placed scattered cross stitches across a plain tent stitch background. The plaid designs in the Plaids and Thistles chapter on page 108 would make wonderful backgrounds for floral or other motifs.

Adding a border

Many counted thread designs look more complete with a border to set them off. It is always best to sketch a border pattern on to squared paper first to make sure that the corners turn correctly. The samplers on pages 82 and 85 have simple geometric wave borders. The one around the Traditional Sampler echoes the small decorative device on the letters, and part of the border design embellishes the numerals.

Choosing a colour scheme

Your choice of colour in a design is influenced by personal preference and also by the décor of your home or the colour of a garment. It affects the appearance of a design so much that it is often difficult to separate the two and imagine how the same composition might look in different colours.

*e*mbroidery threads come in a glorious array of colours, enabling you to put together any colour scheme you choose.

By using totally different colour schemes, very varied effects can be created. For example, to achieve a faded Victorian appearance for a floral pattern, choose muted colours such as grey blues, dusty pinks and earthy greens against a velvety maroon background. In contrast, vivid oranges and brilliant pinks with deep greens on a black background will give the same design a chinoiserie look.

Do experiment with colour. If you find it difficult to choose toning colours, ask at your embroidery shop to see the full shade card for the yarn you are using. You will then find it easier to pick yarns from the same family of colours. Ask, too, if you can check the yarn colours by daylight, as they look quite different under artificial light and you may discover that they are not the exact shades you are looking for.

*t*he plain charcoal background of this cushion has been broken up with a small berry motif.

Changing the size of a design

You may find that you want to change the size of one of the designs in the book to fit a larger or smaller area. For example, you might like to reduce a cushion design to make a small framed picture or even a pin cushion. To do this, you will need to use a different gauge of canvas or evenweave fabric to work on.

A basic rule to remember is that the SMALLER the number of holes to 2.5cm (1in) in your fabric, the LARGER the design will be. To work out in more detail which canvas or fabric to use, divide the number of squares across the chart by the size in inches you want your design to be. This will give you the thread count per inch of the canvas or fabric you need. (Remember that cross stitch is often worked over two threads on fine evenweave fabric, so in this case you will need to double your answer to find the thread count.)

For example, if your chart has 140 squares across and you want your design to be 10 inches wide, you will need a 14-gauge canvas or fabric. If the calculation does not work out to an exact number, you will have to round it up and extend the background slightly.

Have a closer look at some of the motifs in the book which are worked on fabrics and canvases with different thread counts and you will see how different in size they are. The plums on the needlepoint stool on page 33 are worked on an 8-gauge canvas and so have eight stitches to 2.5cm (1in), while the one on the napkin on page 28 has 16 stitches to 2.5cm (1in). The plum on the napkin is therefore half the size each way of the equivalent plum on the stool. Then compare the napkin design with the finely worked plums on the linen tablecloth on page 31. This is made from a 30-count fabric and so here the plums are almost half the size each way again.

There is another calculation you might need to make when designing your own arrangement of motifs from different chapters in the book. You may already have a certain gauge of canvas or fabric in mind and you will then need to know how big your various motifs will look when worked on this particular background. You need to count the number of squares across the width and height of the chart, and also the number of holes per inch in your fabric. For example, if the chart for a fruit motif measures 24 squares wide and 40 squares high and you are using a canvas or fabric with 8 holes to the inch, your motif will measure:

$$24 \div 8 = 3 \text{ inches wide}$$
$$40 \div 8 = 5 \text{ inches high}$$

As mentioned before, with fine evenweave linen you may want to work cross stitch over two threads of the fabric. You will then need to calculate slightly differently. On a 32-count linen, there will be 16 cross stitches to the inch. The fruit motif in the example above will therefore measure:

$$24 \div 16 = 1\tfrac{1}{2} \text{ inches wide}$$
$$40 \div 16 = 2\tfrac{1}{2} \text{ inches high}$$

(If you are calculating in centimetres, there are 2.5cm to the inch.)

*t*he same plum motif is used on the needlepoint stool (top) and on the cross stitch napkin (above). A plum on the stool is 10cm (4in) high, on the napkin only 5cm (2in) high.

OPPOSITE
*t*he size of this bow motif varies considerably depending on the type of canvas or fabric on which it is stitched. The smaller the number of holes to 2.5cm (1in) in your fabric, the larger the motif will be.

*i*f you want to make up your own embroidery design, plan the position of the motifs on paper before you begin stitching, first working out the size that the motifs will be when stitched on to your chosen needlepoint canvas or evenweave fabric. Here I have traced the pears directly from the chart and am transferring the stepped outline to paper. You can make the outline less detailed if you only want a rough positioning guide.

Planning your composition

Once you have worked out the approximate size of your motifs and the gauge of canvas or fabric you need, you can begin to plan your design in more detail. The following guidelines apply whether you are creating your own design or combining motifs from various charts to stitch one of the designs from the book.

Make a rough tracing or drawing of each individual motif in the size it will be when stitched. For tracing purposes, charted designs can be enlarged or reduced to scale if necessary by using a photocopier, but I find that just visualizing how the design will look if larger or smaller is not too difficult.

Transfer the motif on to a plain sheet of paper, which you can cut to the size of your finished project if appropriate. Then draw the next motif to size and transfer it to the

plain paper, positioning it as you wish. You can reverse the design by turning the tracing paper over.

For needlepoint, the main part of your design should be placed in the central area of your canvas. This does not mean that you cannot extend the design outside this area. For example, in the Stool with Plums and Apple project on page 33, the fruits have been placed at the corners of the stool as these are a dominant feature of this particular piece of furniture. However, be aware that a large motif placed too near the edge of a seat will look as though it is falling off and will make the composition appear lop-sided. With a rectangular stool, therefore, place the fruit motifs more centrally.

If you plan your design on paper before you start stitching, it will help you to produce a balanced composition. You can then mark

go over your design with a dark line and place the canvas over the top. You will be able to see the motifs through the canvas and can trace the outlines with an indelible pen.

With evenweave fabric, you could use tailor's chalk as a guide. Alternatively, trace your design on to tissue paper, pin to the fabric and work small tacking stitches around the outlines and through the fabric. Then tear away the tissue paper.

the rough outlines of the motifs on to the canvas or fabric if you wish, so that you know where to begin stitching. Use an HB pencil or indelible marking pen on canvas and tacking threads, tailor's chalk, or a water-erasable marking pen on evenweave fabric.

Beginning to stitch

When I am working on a corner motif, I always stitch from the corner in towards the centre. By doing this, not too much counting is involved, as I need only do a rough thread count from the edge.

When working a central design, I fold my fabric into quarters to find the middle. You can work two lines of tacking stitches to mark the centre more permanently. Find the centre of the chart, too, and begin here, working the design outwards. Again, this reduces too much thread counting.

ABCDE
FGHIJKLMNOP
QRSTUVWXYZ
1234567890
Abigail Saint George
6.11.80

*m*ark the centre of the fabric with horizontal and vertical lines of tacking to help with counting stitches when you are following a chart.

fruit & butterflies

Plump full fruits, ripened under the summer sun, offer a wonderful subject for needlepoint and cross stitch with their dappled skins and rich autumnal colours. Butterflies, moths and shimmering dragonflies are also endlessly satisfying to create in embroidery and the combination of these delicate creatures with the heavy ripe fruit makes a winning formula. It is fascinating to see the very different effects which can be achieved by changing the scale in embroidery, and I have illustrated this by using the fruit motifs on the following pages on a wide range of fabrics from a fine closely woven linen to an eight-gauge canvas.

*l*ustrous embroidery cottons are used for the fruits and butterflies on this elegant chair and tablecloth – an inviting combination for afternoon tea.

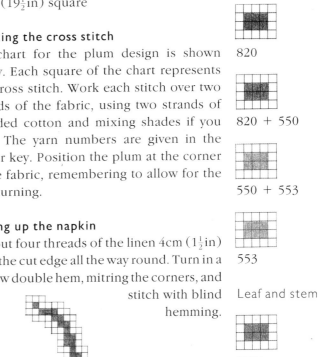

p l u m   n a p k i n

The cross stitch plum on this linen napkin was designed to echo the fruit on a favourite set of tea cups. Fine china is a rich source of ideas for motifs which you can embroider on to table linen to match your favourite tea-set or dinner service.

I achieved the lustrous sheen of a ripened plum by combining different shades of stranded cotton. At the darker outer edges I used two strands of purple. Moving inwards, I mixed one strand of purple with one strand of blue to give subtle shading. Then I used two strands of blue and for the highlight I mixed the blue with violet.

Size

46cm (18in) square

Yarns

DMC stranded cotton
One skein each of the following colours:
Plum
Purples and blue (dark to light)
820, 550, 553
Leaf and stem
Greens (dark to light) 890, 3345, 987
Brown 3781

Other materials

For one napkin, piece of 32-count evenweave linen which measures about 50cm (19½in) square

Working the cross stitch

The chart for the plum design is shown below. Each square of the chart represents one cross stitch. Work each stitch over two threads of the fabric, using two strands of stranded cotton and mixing shades if you wish. The yarn numbers are given in the colour key. Position the plum at the corner of the fabric, remembering to allow for the hem turning.

Making up the napkin

Pull out four threads of the linen 4cm (1½in) from the cut edge all the way round. Turn in a narrow double hem, mitring the corners, and stitch with blind hemming.

Plum

820

820 + 550

550 + 553

553

Leaf and stem

3781

890

3345

987

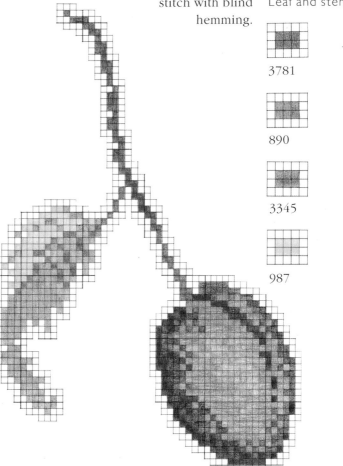

p ears and plums tablecloth

Pears and stem

898

840

420

422

725

3078

Pear leaves

500

367

320

These fruits decorating the corner of a linen tablecloth have 30 stitches to 2.5cm (1in) – very fine and delicate work. It is not too good for the eyesight, but I was curious to see the effect and I enjoy a small amount of close work. I used half cross stitch with only two strands of stranded cotton for the tiny stitches. The fruit composition has a patina of age which I achieved using a muted palette of colours.

It is interesting to contrast this minutely worked fruit with the bold version stitched in tapestry wool on the Stool with Plums and Apple on page 34, as this gives you each end of the spectrum of sizes you can achieve while using the same pattern.

OPPOSITE
$t$he finely worked stitches give the fruit a slightly embossed effect.

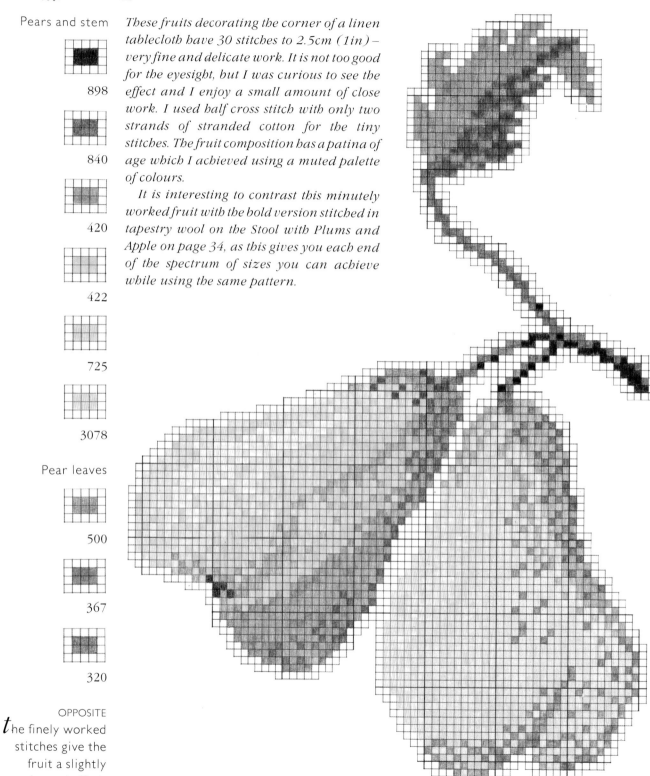

Size
100cm (39in) square

Yarns
DMC stranded cotton
One skein each of the following colours:
Pears
Browns (dark to light) 898, 840, 420, 422
Yellows (dark to light) 725, 3078
Pear leaves
Greens (dark to light) 500, 367, 320
Plums
Crimsons (dark to light) 902, 326, 309, 223
Plum leaves
Greens (dark to light) 500, 501, 561
Stems
Browns (dark to light) 898, 840

Other materials
Piece of 30-count evenweave linen
measuring 108cm (42in) square

*t*he delicate
stitching of the fruit
(below) contrasts
vividly with the
bolder approach
used on the
triangular stool
(opposite).

Working the embroidery
The fruit designs are taken from the charts
shown on pages 30 and 36–7. Each square of
the charts represents one half cross stitch.
Work each stitch over one thread of the
fabric, using two strands of stranded cotton.

The yarn numbers for the pears are given
in the colour key with the pears chart. The
yarn numbers given in the key for the plums
chart refer specifically to the colours used in
the Stool with Plums and Apple project.
Substitute the stranded cotton colours listed
above when following this chart. To help
with positioning the motifs, refer to the
photographs of the tablecloth or arrange the
fruit as you wish.

Making up the tablecloth
Turn up a 2cm ($\frac{3}{4}$in) double hem all round,
mitring the corners, and stitch down neatly
with blind hemming.

*d*ramatic colour and a large-gauge canvas combine to make this stunning triangular stool an exciting project to stitch in soft tapestry wools.

S tool with plums and apple

a lthough this is an ambitious project, it works up relatively quickly in chunky tent stitches on a large-gauge canvas.

This unusual triangular stool lent itself to a dramatic treatment. I used large-gauge canvas to give a bold effect, and placed the fruit at each corner, positioning the stems and leaves to link the plums and apple into a cohesive design. The rich red of the apple and the purple and blue of the plums glow against the black background.

In using the fruit motifs for different projects in this chapter, I have cheated somewhat, as the shape of the peach and the apple and their leaves are similar. The fruit shape I have taken here as an apple is basically the same as the one I have used as a peach on the Butterfly and Fruit Chair on page 42. Only the colours are different – strong reds instead of beige and pink. One could also
interpret the plums in different colours – purples, maroons, greens or yellows.

Size
The stool illustrated measures approximately 58cm (23in) along each side

Yarns
DMC 4-ply tapestry wool (listed from dark to light):
I have not given yarn quantities here as this will vary depending on the size of your stool. To estimate how much yarn you might need, refer to page 12.
Apple
Reds 7110, 7107, 7849, 7666

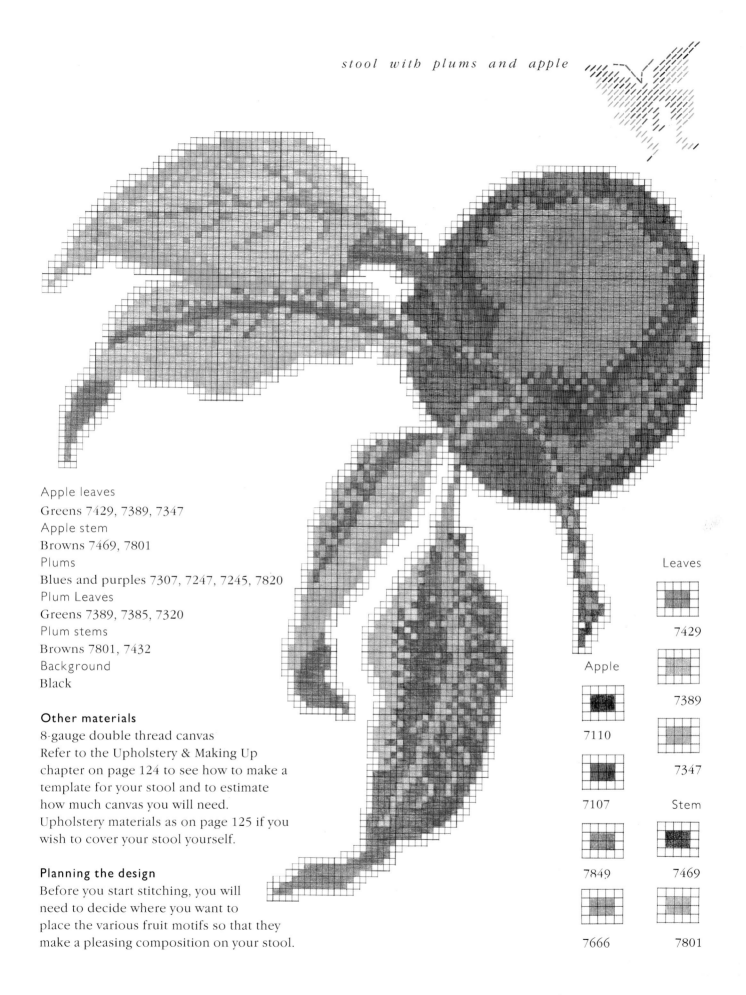

Apple leaves
Greens 7429, 7389, 7347
Apple stem
Browns 7469, 7801
Plums
Blues and purples 7307, 7247, 7245, 7820
Plum Leaves
Greens 7389, 7385, 7320
Plum stems
Browns 7801, 7432
Background
Black

Other materials

8-gauge double thread canvas
Refer to the Upholstery & Making Up
chapter on page 124 to see how to make a
template for your stool and to estimate
how much canvas you will need.
Upholstery materials as on page 125 if you
wish to cover your stool yourself.

Planning the design

Before you start stitching, you will
need to decide where you want to
place the various fruit motifs so that they
make a pleasing composition on your stool.

Leaves

7429

7389

7347

Apple

7110

7107

Stem

7849   7469

7666   7801

Stems

7801

7432

Plums

7307

7247

7245

7820

Refer to page 24 and to the photographs shown here to help you with planning the design.

Working the needlepoint

The fruit motifs are shown on the charts on page 35 and on these two pages. Each square of the charts represents one tent stitch. The yarn numbers are given in the colour key. Select the areas of the charts which are relevant to your design.

Making up the stool

Stretch the needlepoint back into shape if necessary (see stretching instructions on page 1/). Instructions on how to upholster a stool are given in the Upholstery & Making Up chapter on page 124. Alternatively, you may wish to have your stool professionally upholstered.

Leaves

7389

7385

7320

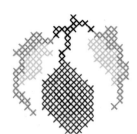

b u t t e r f l y   c u r t a i n

The butterflies on these light muslin curtains gleam against the light as if they have just fluttered in through the window and alighted on the fabric. I positioned the lustrous dragonfly and the misty moth with their darker tones lower down on the curtain and the paler butterflies high above them to emphasize the elegant proportions of the French doors. You can choose just one or two butterflies or many more to suit the style of your curtains, and, using the waste canvas method, you can position them wherever you like and at any angle.

Size
To suit your own window

Yarns
DMC stranded cotton
One skein each of the following colours:
Dragonfly
820 dark blue, 792 mid blue,
890 forest green, 3362 sage green

Moth
552 dark violet, 553 mid violet,
792 mid blue, 3362 sage green
Swallowtail butterfly
792 mid blue, 809 sky blue, 3747 pale blue,
553 mid violet, 3362 sage green
Small butterfly
809 sky blue, 3747 pale blue,
818 pale pink, 3362 sage green
Turning butterfly
899 dark pink, 776 mid pink, 818 pale pink,
799 bluebell

Other materials
Lightweight cotton or muslin to fit your window plus heading and hem allowances.
9-gauge waste canvas

Turning butterfly

899

776

818

799

Small butterfly

809

3747

818

3362

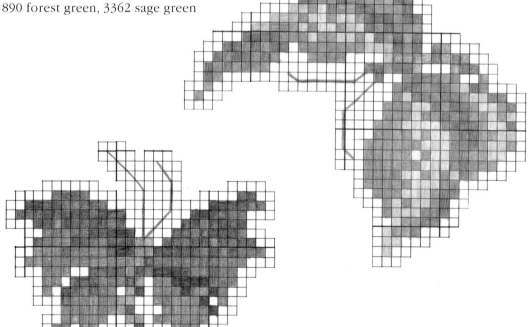

*l*ike a breath of summer, butterflies are captured in all their glory on the billowing curtain. Light filters through their fluttering bodies on the translucent muslin fabric.

39

*t*he butterflies were worked on to the lightweight fabric using waste canvas. With this technique it is easy to achieve the most subtle effects with a delectable choice of cotton threads.

Working the cross stitch

The charts for the butterfly designs are shown on pages 38 and 41. Each square of the charts represents one cross stitch.

Decide where you wish to position each butterfly and tack a piece of waste canvas at this point. The waste canvas should be cut to the following sizes for the various motifs:
Dragonfly 21 × 12cm ($8\frac{1}{2}$ × $4\frac{1}{2}$in)
Moth 18 × 13cm (7 × 5in)
Swallowtail butterfly 14cm ($5\frac{1}{2}$in) square
Small butterfly 12 × 9cm ($4\frac{1}{2}$ × $3\frac{1}{2}$in)
Turning butterfly 13 × 12cm (5 × $4\frac{1}{2}$in).
Work the cross stitch over the waste canvas, using three strands of stranded cotton. The yarn numbers are given in the colour keys. When each motif is complete,

remove the waste canvas as described on page 16.

Making up the curtain

Turn in a 1.5cm ($\frac{1}{2}$in) double hem along the sides of the curtain. Add a heading tape of your choice and turn up a double 7.5cm (3in) hem at the bottom of the curtain.

butterfly curtain

Swallowtail butterfly

792

809

3747

553

3362

Moth

552

553

792

3362

Dragonfly

820

792

890

3362

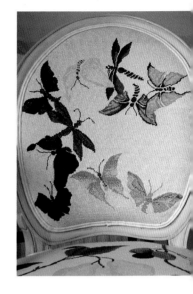

butterfly and fruit chair

This luxurious chair, shimmering in pearl cottons, is an ambitious project but worth the effort for the magnificent result. It is a design which is full of light and movement. I placed the heavy ripe fruit on the seat of the chair with the light butterflies hovering above on the chair back. Each time I enter the room, it seems as if I have disturbed the butterflies which fly off, unfurling their radiant colours.

I chose pearl cottons for this needlepoint as I was fascinated by the wealth of colours, gleaming like silk. Having planned out my design, I actually stencilled the butterflies and fruit on to the canvas and enjoyed playing with the paint tones in order to achieve a feeling of movement. I then stitched over the motifs with the pearl cotton, filling in the background afterwards.

You can work out a design to suit your shape of chair and then either mark the motifs on to the canvas as I did, or stitch the combination of butterflies and fruit from the charts provided. I found the work compelling, and while I listened for hours to my young children reading aloud, I finished the seat, the armrests and then the back as their reading improved.

Size
The chair back measures 42cm ($16\frac{1}{2}$in) high by 35cm (14in) wide
The chair seat measures 62cm ($24\frac{1}{2}$in) deep by 66cm (26in) wide
The armrests measure 19cm ($7\frac{1}{2}$in) long and 12cm ($4\frac{3}{4}$in) wide

Yarns
DMC coton perlé No. 5
I have not given yarn quantities here as this will vary depending on the size of your chair. To estimate how much yarn you might need, refer to page 12.
Background
Ecru

Butterflies, moths, dragonflies and fruit
Blues (dark to light) 820, 792, 799, 827
Purples (dark to light) 550, 552, 553
Yellows (dark to light) 444, 307, 445, 745
Greens (dark to light) 890, 936, 699, 904, 911, 905, 907
Browns and beiges (dark to light) 3371, 839, 840, 842, 739
Pinks (dark to light) 3350, 602, 956, 225, 948, 818

Other materials
15-gauge mono canvas
Refer to the Upholstery & Making Up chapter on page 124 to see how to make a template for your chair and to estimate how much canvas you will need.

Planning the design
Before you start stitching, you will need to decide where you want to place the various fruit and butterfly motifs so that they make a pleasing composition on your chair. Refer to page 24 and to the photographs shown here to help you with planning the design and let your imagination run riot.

Working the needlepoint
The charts for the fruit and butterfly motifs are shown throughout this chapter. Each square of the charts represents one tent stitch. The yarn numbers for the peach enclosed by leaves are given in the colour key on page 45. The yarn numbers given in the other colour keys refer specifically to the projects in which they appear. For this Butterfly and Fruit Chair project, use the colours listed above for the various motifs or substitute colours to match your décor.

OPPOSITE AND ABOVE
*n*ot a project for the faint-hearted, this splendid chair is worked entirely in tent stitch in pearl cottons. The chair has attracted many admirers and continues to give me intense pleasure.

*t*his chart shows one of the peach motifs enclosed by leaves.

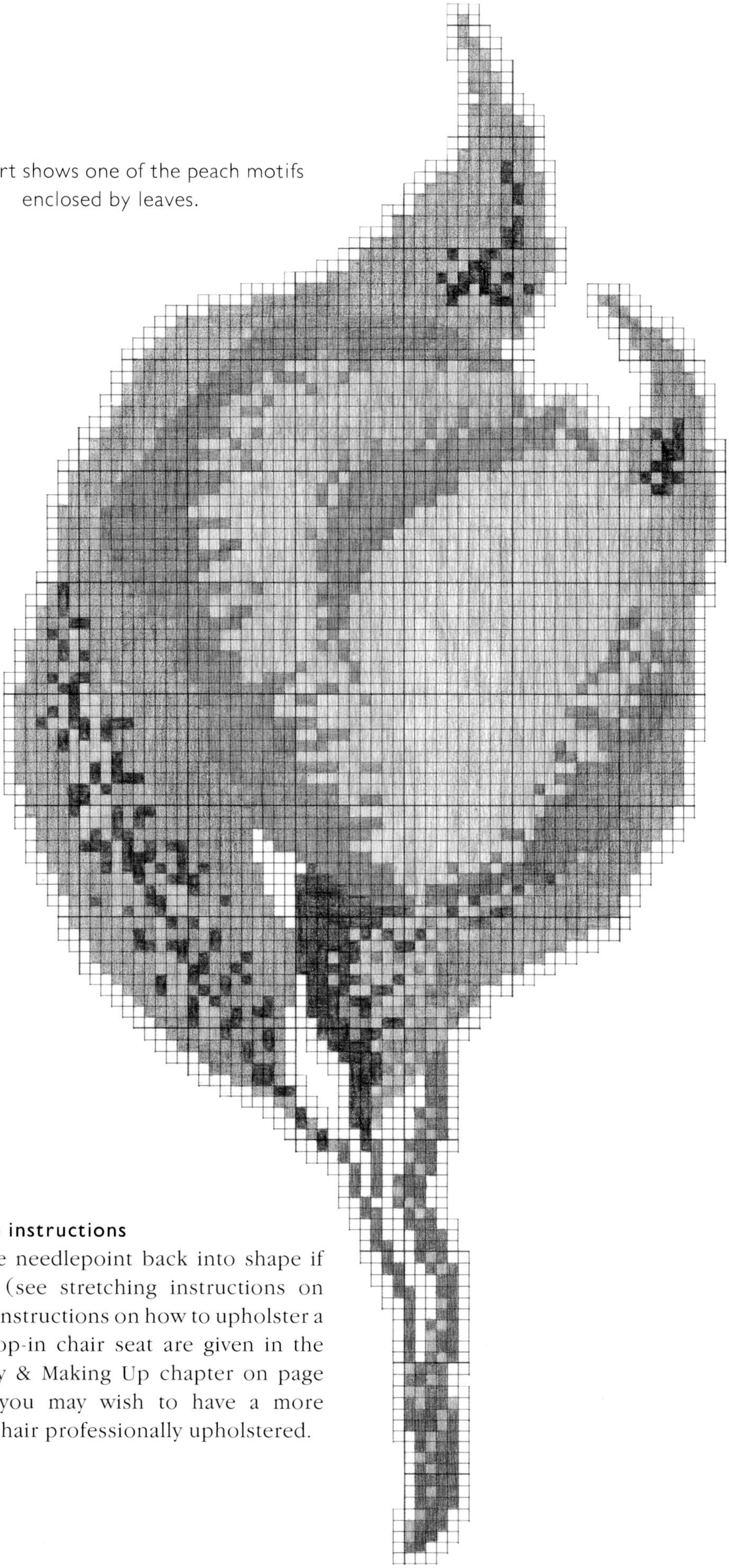

Peach

842

739

745

Leaves

699

904

911

Stem

3371

840

Making up instructions

Stretch the needlepoint back into shape if necessary (see stretching instructions on page 17.) Instructions on how to upholster a simple drop-in chair seat are given in the Upholstery & Making Up chapter on page 124, but you may wish to have a more complex chair professionally upholstered.

OPPOSITE

*t*his detail shows the delicacy and lustre of the stitching. The arrangement of fruits gives a wonderful feeling of movement with the butterfly hovering in anticipation.

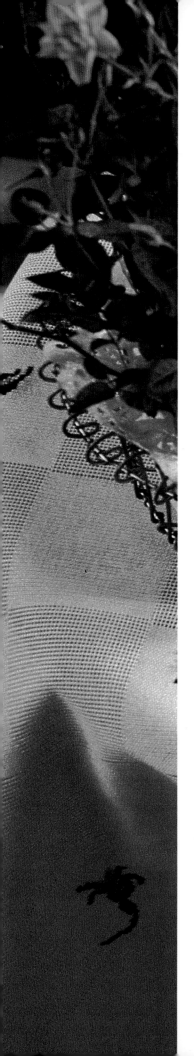

roses & buds

the rose is a timeless image for decoration in the home and has been used by generation after generation to symbolize perfection in a flower. In full bloom or in a tightly furled bud, roses lend themselves particularly well to embroidery and are very versatile. A fresh-looking single rose strewn on to a cushion will fit into any décor, while buds can make up a geometric border pattern or be scattered at random over table linen. You need not restrict your choice of colours when embroidering roses – whether blending with nature or tinted with a touch of imagination, the rose makes a beautiful motif to interpret as you please.

*a*bundant roses in needlepoint on a chair cushion and delicate buds in cross stitch on a tablecloth show the versatility of these flower motifs for all kinds of home furnishings.

r ose-bud trestle

I found this inexpensive lightweight mahogany trestle tucked away in a flea market and have been amused to see the variety of uses to which it has been put so far, ranging from a stand for a tea-tray to a luggage rack at the end of a guest bed. The little trestle folds away neatly when not in use.

Needlepoint, while its patterning may look delicate, is actually very strong, so it is the ideal technique to use for these trestle braces which need to withstand a certain amount of strain. I have used the rose-bud motif in a simple traditional manner, reversing and repeating it along the bands. So that I could move the trestle from one room to another, I needed quite subtle colours to match different decorating schemes, so I chose yellow buds which would go well both in my blue bedroom and the natural browns of a guest room. And the repeating bud pattern looks formal enough for the trestle to be used in the sitting room next to a mainly black sofa. I incorporated a frame design behind the bud for depth.

Size
The straps measure 59 × 6cm (23 × 2¼in)

Yarns
DMC 4-ply tapestry wool
Petals and frames
Yellows (dark to light)
Two skeins each of 7727, 7905
Leaves and stems
Greens (dark to light)
Two skeins each of 7890 and 7768,
one skein of 7770
Background
Six skeins of black

Other materials
Two pieces of 10-gauge double thread canvas measuring 69 × 16cm (27 × 6¼in)
Webbing for backing the straps
A few tacks

Working the needlepoint
The chart for the rose-bud design is shown on this page. Each square of the chart represents one needlepoint stitch. So that the straps would not be too thick, I used half cross stitch for this project. The yarn numbers are given in the colour key.

Start stitching at one end of the strap, leaving a 5cm (2in) border of unworked canvas all round. Roll up the excess length of canvas and secure it. Stitch the bud motifs first, then the background. As you progress, gradually unroll the unworked canvas and roll up the part you have finished. This will keep your work clean and will also help to prevent the canvas from distorting.

Making up the straps
Turn under the unworked canvas edges. Stitch on the webbing at the back. Then attach the straps to the trestle frame with the tacks, rolling the unfinished canvas underneath out of sight.

*t*his trestle is very adaptable around the home. Do experiment with simple designs, as they can be so effective.

Petals

7727

7905

Leaves and stems

7890

7768

7770

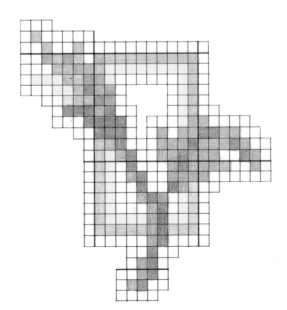

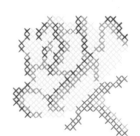

*y*ellow rose cushion

*d*etails of the cushion (above) and the chart (below) show how the coloured squares translate into stitches.

A single perfect rose is a design motif which blends into all settings, especially when you choose a colour to tone with your interior. I love solitary flowers and have a single dried rose, gathered from a summer walk, resting on my desk top.

The sunny yellow rose worked in cross stitch on this charming cushion retains all the freshness of a newly picked bloom. A stem of rose-buds balances this design as it is worked on a square background, but this could be omitted on items with a different shape. For a cushion that smells as delightful as it looks, it is a nice idea to sew a muslin bag of pot pourri into the cushion pad, bringing the scent of the garden indoors.

If your décor is already floral, whether on your furnishing fabrics or wallpaper, the occasional scatter cushion with a rose motif can echo this, placed in amongst plain cushions on a sofa or bed. So many designs require a lot of thought when combining several elements, but the single rose is delightfully easy and can be placed on many other linens and furnishings around the home, such as sheets, pillowcases, tablecloths and throws.

Size
30.5cm (12in) square

Yarns
DMC stranded cotton
One skein each of the following colours:
Petals
Golds and yellows (dark to light)
680, 743, 3046, 3047
Leaves and stem
Greens (dark to light) 500, 890, 936
Brown 938

Other materials
Piece of 14-count oatmeal Aida fabric measuring 46cm (18in) square
Piece of backing fabric measuring 33cm (13in) square
140cm (55in) thick piping cord
140cm (55in) yellow bias binding
Cushion pad measuring 33cm (13in) square

Working the cross stitch
The chart for the rose design is shown on page 52. Each square of the chart represents one cross stitch. Work each cross stitch over one block of the Aida fabric, using three strands of stranded cotton throughout. The yarn numbers are given in the colour key.

Making up the cushion
Make up as for a piped cushion on page 126, adding a zip at the back if required. If you would like to add a little muslin bag of pot pourri for a scented cushion, you could sew your own cushion pad and insert the bag with the stuffing.

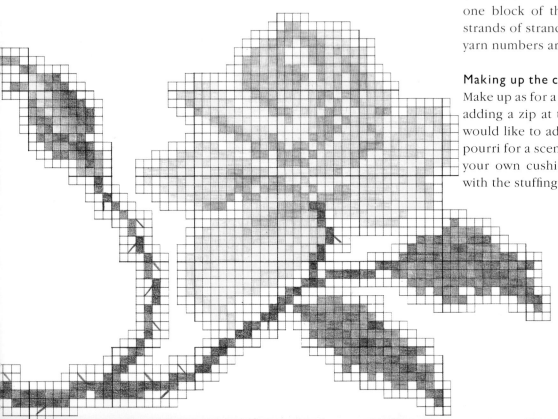

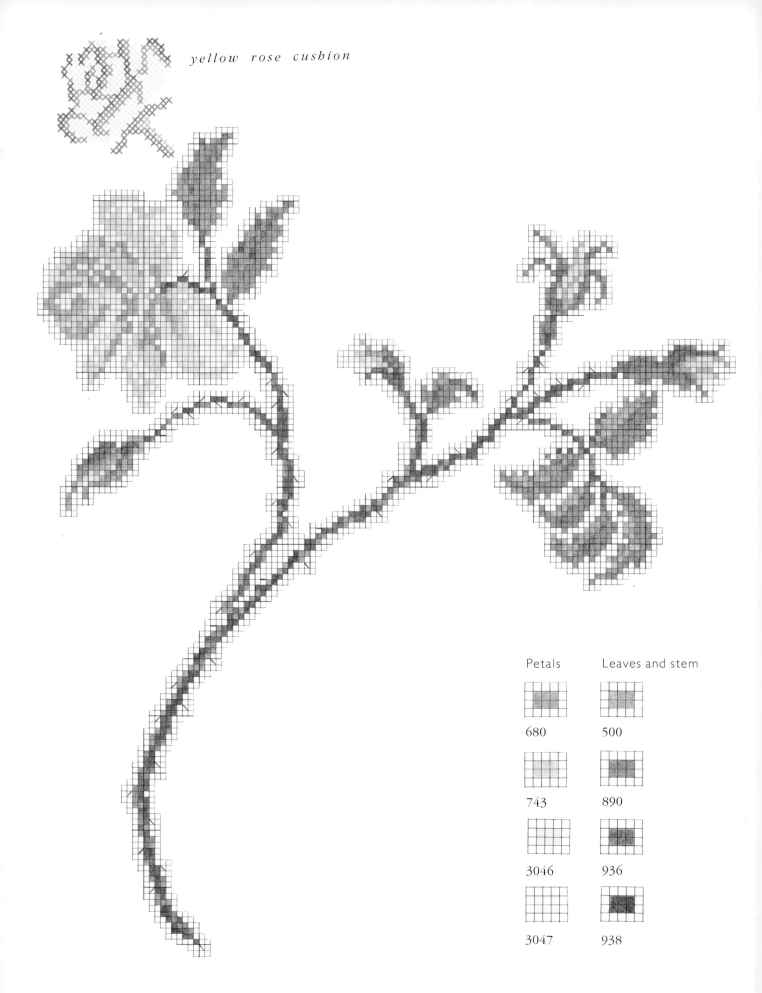

yellow rose cushion

Petals

680	

743

3046

3047

Leaves and stem

500

890

936

938

*r*ose-buds dance over the chequered weave of this tablecloth, the stems trailing in all directions to add rhythm to the design. It is a wonderful cloth for a wedding or christening table.

r ose-bud tablecloth

The chequered evenweave cotton I chose for this tablecloth was a delightful fabric to work with. I wondered at first if I would find the little squares confining, but not at all. I used four rose-bud designs and added variety by placing them differently and trailing their stems at random for movement. The buds can curve to the left or the right, and can be worked upwards or downwards, giving you four ways of using the same motif.

When you are working motifs in different directions on the cloth, you may have a problem getting all the cross stitches going the same way. To overcome this, I made one huge cross stitch in the middle of the cloth and always referred to it from whichever side I was working, unpicking it later.

The colours of the buds were chosen to tone with the plates in the photograph. You may like to follow this idea and match the thread colours to your own china.

Size
To suit your table. The tablecloth illustrated measures 130cm (51in) square

Yarns
DMC stranded cotton
For 36 rose-buds, one skein each of the following colours:
Petals
Pinks (dark to light) 899, 776, 819
Leaves and stems
Greens (dark to light) 890, 3345, 987
Brown 3790

Other materials
Length of 28-count chequered evenweave fabric to suit your table

Working the cross stitch
The charts for the rose-buds are shown on pages 49 and 52. Each square of the charts represents one cross stitch. Work each cross stitch over two threads of the fabric, using three strands of the stranded cotton. Use the colours listed above if you want pink buds or substitute colours of your choice.

Place the buds at random or, if you prefer,

*t*he rose-buds sprinkled over the cloth harmonize with the pattern on the china to give a coordinated look to the table setting.

in a formal arrangement such as chequer-board fashion, in straight rows, as a dominant central feature or simply around the outer edge of the tablecloth.

Making up the tablecloth
To finish off the edges, turn up a 2.5cm (1in) double hem all round the tablecloth, mitring the corners.

Sewing roll and pin cushion

If there is a glimpse of sun I work outside, taking all my sewing requirements with me, so I like everything I work with to be easily transportable. My work-basket invariably stays in the cupboard as I find the convenience of having just a few accessories to hand in this simple sewing roll less compli-cated. In it I keep my embroidery scissors, a selection of needles tucked into an attached piece of felt, the skeins of thread that I am using on my current project and the tiny pin cushion. The pin cushion is stuffed with sawdust which, my grandmother assures me, is the traditional way to keep pins shiny.

The sewing roll is made up in white Aida fabric lined with pale blue, and is edged with navy rickrack braid. On opening the roll, a sprig of leaves and the little pin cushion are revealed. This is an ideal project for a beginner as the motifs are simple and the fabric is easy to work with.

Size
Open sewing roll: 24 × 14cm ($9\frac{1}{2}$ × $5\frac{1}{2}$in)
Pin cushion: 7 × 5cm ($2\frac{3}{4}$ × 2in)

Yarns
DMC stranded cotton
One skein each of the following colours:
Petals
Blues (dark to light) 312, 775
Leaves and stems
Greens (dark to light) 890, 987, 368

Other materials
One blue and one white piece of 14-count
Aida fabric, each measuring 34cm ($13\frac{1}{2}$in)
square
Piece of white felt measuring 11 × 9cm
($4\frac{1}{2}$ × $3\frac{1}{2}$in)
85cm ($33\frac{1}{2}$in) navy rickrack braid
Handful of sawdust to stuff pin cushion

Petals

312

775

Leaves and stem

890

987

368

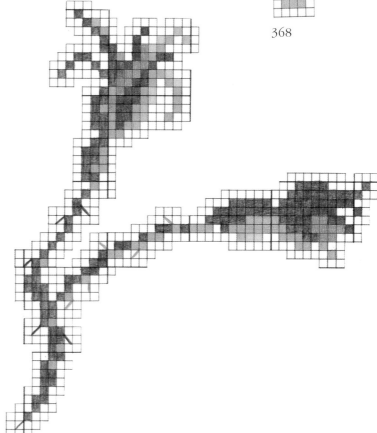

$\mathcal{W}$ork-in-progress on a blue cross stitch collar for my daughter, Tiphaine. I find the little sewing roll spread out on my work table convenient to have to hand.

Working the cross stitch

The designs for the rose-buds and the sprig of leaves are taken from the charts on pages 52 and 57 respectively. Each square of the charts represents one cross stitch. Work each cross stitch over one block of fabric, using three strands of stranded cotton throughout. The yarn numbers for the rose-buds are given in the colour key. For the leaves, use the greens listed on page 57.

Work the rose-buds on the white fabric and the sprig of leaves on the blue fabric, taking care with their positioning. Work a single rose-bud on the white fabric for the little pin cushion.

Making up the sewing roll

Trim the white and blue fabrics to 26 × 16cm ($10\frac{1}{2}$ × $6\frac{1}{2}$in). Stitch the felt to the blue lining fabric along the left-hand fold, just below the leaf design. Stitch the blue and white fabrics together, right sides facing, with a 1cm ($\frac{1}{2}$in) turning, catching in the rickrack. Leave an opening for turning through. Turn through and sew up the opening by hand.

Making up the pin cushion

Trim the white and blue fabrics to 9 × 7cm ($3\frac{3}{4}$ × 3in). Stitch the back and front together as for the sewing roll, inserting the sawdust stuffing through the opening.

*l*avish pink roses decorate this inviting chair cushion. The needlepoint design would also look beautiful on a drop-in chair seat.

pink rose chair cushion

roses are very versatile motifs which can be used singly or gathered into sprays or bouquets, giving lots of scope for creative design ideas.

This needlepoint chair cushion shows the rose motifs used in all their glorious forms from opulent full-blown flower head to delicate bud. A set of chair cushions, each with a different arrangement of roses, would look superb in the dining room, or you could use the design on a drop-in chair seat.

Size
The chair cushion illustrated measures approximately 40cm (16in) deep and 47cm (18½in) at the front edge

Yarns
DMC tapestry wool
I have not given yarn quantities here as this will vary depending on the size of your chair. To estimate how much yarn you might need, refer to page 12.
Petals
Pinks (dark to light) 7544, 7849, 7104, 7103
Leaves and stems
Greens (dark to light) 7347, 7346, 7344
Browns (dark to light) 7479, 7845
Background
7853

Other materials
10-gauge double thread canvas
If you are making a chair cushion, measure your chair seat and allow an extra 5cm (2in) all round to find the canvas size.
Piece of backing fabric to match canvas
Braid trim
Cushion pad to fit
If you wish to make a drop-in chair seat, refer to the Upholstery & Making Up chapter on page 124 to see how to make a pattern and to estimate how much canvas you will need.
Upholstery materials as on page 125 if you wish to cover your chair seat yourself.

Planning the design
Before you start stitching, you will need to decide where you want to place the various rose motifs so that they make a pleasing composition on your chair seat. Refer to page 24 and to the photograph on page 59 to help you with planning the design.

Working the needlepoint
The rose motifs are shown on the charts opposite and on page 52. Each square of the charts represents one tent stitch. The yarn numbers for the pair of pink roses are given in the colour key with this chart. The yarn numbers given in the key with the Yellow Rose Cushion chart refer specifically to that project, so substitute the colours listed above or colours of your choice.

Making up the chair seats
Stretch the needlepoint back into shape if necessary (see stretching instructions on page 17). Make up the cushion as on page 126, adding braid if required. Alternatively, instructions on how to upholster a simple drop-in chair seat are given in the Upholstery & Making Up chapter on page 124, but you may wish to have your chair professionally upholstered.

Petals

7544

7849

7104

7103

Leaves and stems

7347

7346

7344

7479

7845

ribbons & bows

ibbons and bows are decorative elements which add the finishing touch to anything from gift-wrapped parcels to festive clothing and hair-styles. They symbolize all the joyous family occasions such as birthdays, weddings, Christmas and Easter, when ribbons tied around flowers, evergreen foliage, chocolate eggs and special cakes dress them up for a celebration.

With their decorative appeal, ribbons and bows are perfect motifs for embroidery and they can be interpreted in so many ways. Bows can be used singly or in groups, while ribbons can twist, overlap or meander alone. They look equally effective in needlepoint or cross stitch and are attractive worked in shiny threads or wools.

Streaming out across the cushion, the ribbons intertwine around a dragonfly and moth in a glorious array of colours.

n ightdress with bow

This pretty single bow, embroidered in cross stitch on a simple nightdress, picks out the cream shade of the buttons and straps. It transforms a plain garment into one which is both elegant and personal.

Quick to work over waste canvas, the bow motif can be used to decorate all kinds of garments. It can soften the look of hard-wearing denim or add an individual touch to a pocket or lapel. A row of bow motifs would look charming around the hem of a child's skirt. Alternatively, if worked in metallic thread, it would add the finishing touch to an evening bag.

Size
The bow motif measures approximately 6.5cm (2½in) high and 7.5cm (3in) wide

Yarns
DMC stranded cotton
One skein each of the following colours:
3047 beige, blanc, écru

Other materials
Plain nightdress
11-gauge waste canvas

*t*his delicate bow is a quick and easy way to personalize a garment. It is worked on to the satin nightdress over waste canvas.

Working the cross stitch
The chart for the bow design is shown on the left. Each square of the chart represents one cross stitch.

Decide where you wish to place the bow and tack a piece of waste canvas measuring 11.5 × 12.5cm (4½ × 5in) at this position. Work the cross stitch over the waste canvas, using three strands of stranded cotton. The yarn numbers are given in the colour key. When the embroidery is complete, remove the waste canvas as described on page 16.

3047

blanc

écru

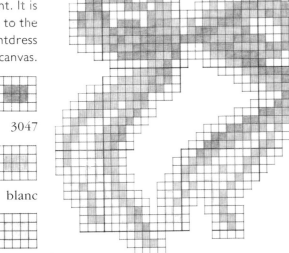

*b*ed linen with trailing ribbons

These wide ribbons unfurl with gay abandon across a simple white cotton duvet cover and pillowcase. I chose vibrant pinks rather than pastels to emphasize the strong design, and the result is a bold pattern which is more appropriate to the large area of plain fabric than a pale dainty ribbon would be. The design would work equally well on the turn-back of a sheet.

On folding back the duvet cover, my cross-stitched initials are revealed. It is pleasing to personalize your embroidery in this way and you can add a date, too, as a reminder of when you completed the project.

As the fabric for the bed linen is too fine for the threads to be counted, the cross stitch ribbons are worked over waste canvas, which is removed from under the stitching once the embroidery is finished.

*W*orked over waste canvas, these ribbons twist and twirl in vivid pinks on classic white cotton bed linen. I added my initials to the duvet cover.

Size
The designs shown are worked on a double duvet cover and a large pillowcase measuring 77cm (30in) square. The ribbon design would also fit on a single duvet

Yarns
DMC stranded cotton
Two skeins each of the following colours:
Cerise pink (dark to light) 600, 602, 603, 605
Pale pink (dark to light) 604, 605, 818, 819

Other materials
Plain duvet cover or sheet and pillowcase
11-gauge waste canvas

67

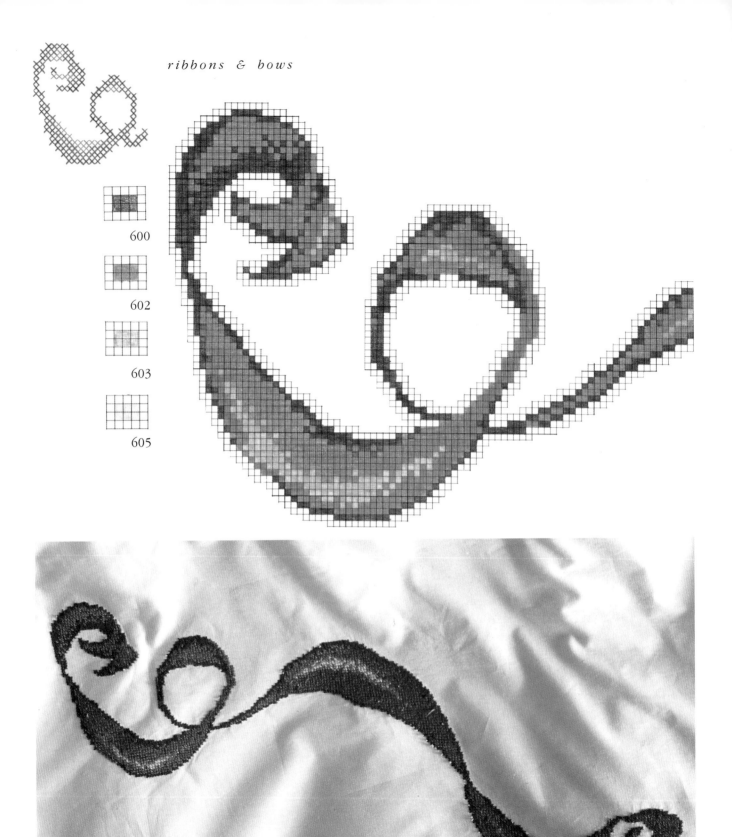

600

602

603

605

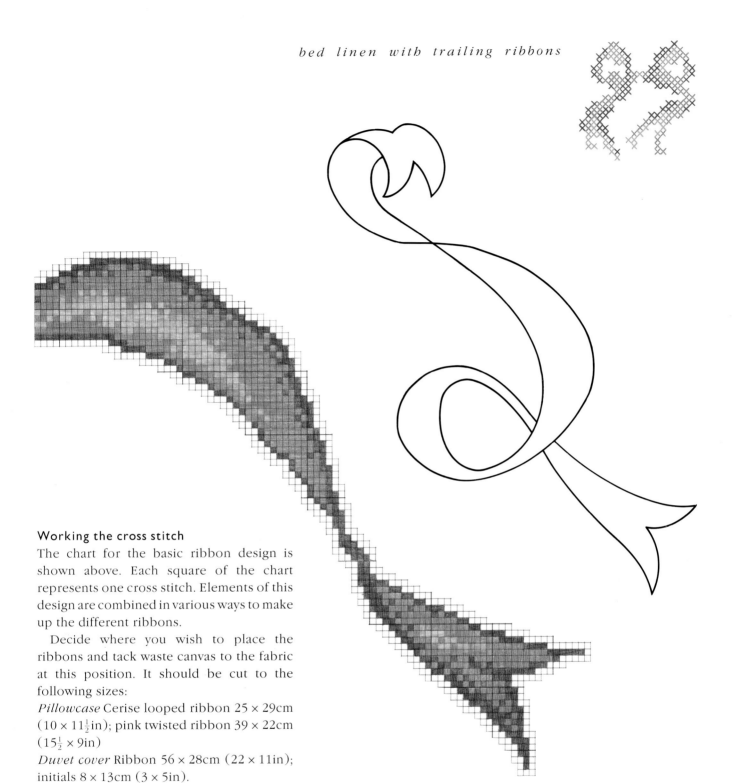

Working the cross stitch

The chart for the basic ribbon design is shown above. Each square of the chart represents one cross stitch. Elements of this design are combined in various ways to make up the different ribbons.

Decide where you wish to place the ribbons and tack waste canvas to the fabric at this position. It should be cut to the following sizes:

Pillowcase Cerise looped ribbon 25 × 29cm (10 × 11½in); pink twisted ribbon 39 × 22cm (15½ × 9in)

Duvet cover Ribbon 56 × 28cm (22 × 11in); initials 8 × 13cm (3 × 5in).

Work the cross stitch over the waste canvas, using three strands of stranded cotton. The yarn numbers for the ribbon on the duvet cover are given in the colour key. On the pillowcase, the looped ribbon is worked in the same cerise colours, while the twisted ribbon is worked in pale pinks. When the motifs are complete, remove the waste canvas as described on page 16.

*t*he chart and diagram (above) show two ways of combining the elements of the trailing ribbon design, but you will discover even more. Remember that the twists and curls can also be stitched as mirror images.

tablecloth with bows and roses

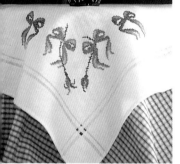

On this small tablecloth I have used bows in combination with two rose-bud motifs from the Yellow Rose Cushion on page 50 in the Roses & Buds chapter. Worked in cross stitch, the four bows are arranged each side of the corner, as mirror images of each other. The buds caught into the bows add charm and interest to the design.

I chose colours to coordinate with the checked tablecloth beneath. If you wish to match a particular tablecloth, change the shades of embroidery thread accordingly. As a finishing touch, I pulled a double row of threads from around the edge of the linen cloth to make a border.

Size

The tablecloth illustrated measures 92cm ($36\frac{1}{4}$in) square

Yarns

DMC stranded cotton
To work the motifs on one corner of the cloth, one skein each of the following colours:
Blues (dark to light) 799, 809, 3747
Greens (dark to light) 987, 522, 368

*t*hese bows make an effective corner motif and could be continued around the edge of the tablecloth if you wish. I have added trailing rose-buds held by the knot of the bows.

Other materials

Piece of 22-count Hardanger fabric measuring 96cm (38in) square

Working the cross stitch

The charts for the bow and rose-bud designs are shown below and on page 52 respectively. Each square of the charts represents one cross stitch. Work each cross stitch over two threads of the Hardanger fabric, using three strands of stranded cotton.

The yarn numbers for the blue bow are given in the colour key. For the green bow, follow the same chart but substitute greens for blues. Similarly, for the rose-buds, substitute the blues listed above for the colours referred to in the colour key.

Positioning the bows and rose-buds

Fold and tack the fabric diagonally through the corners and position the bows either side of the diagonal lines, with the bottom of each bow about 13cm (5in) from the edge of the fabric.

Refer to the photographs shown here to help with positioning the rose-buds. Make the stems look longer than on the charts and link them with the bows.

Making up the tablecloth

Pull a double line of threads from around the evenweave fabric, 8cm (3in) and 9.5cm ($3\frac{3}{4}$in) in from the edge. Turn under a 1cm ($\frac{3}{8}$in) double hem, mitring the corners.

799

809

3747

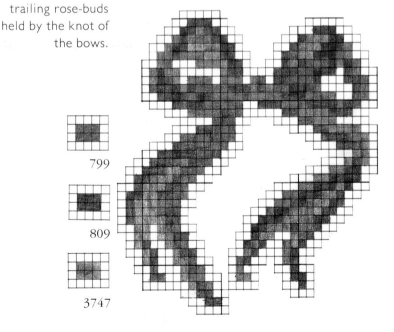

r ed bow footstool

This bold little footstool is tied up with a large needlepoint bow to make a 'present' for your feet to rest on. I have used bright crimson tapestry wool for the bow and ribbon design to make a strong contrast with the cream background.

The basic bow shape is repeated twice, one motif across the other, to form a rosette. It is worked in cross stitch for extra texture and strength, while the background is worked in tent stitch with scattered red cross stitches to add interest to what would otherwise be a large area of plain colour.

Size
The footstool illustrated is an oval measuring 42cm (16½in) long, 33cm (13in) wide and 5cm (2in) deep

Yarns
DMC 4-ply tapestry wool
Bow and ribbons
Three skeins each of the following colours:
Crimsons (dark to light)
7110, 7137, 7107, 7849
Background
Four large background skeins of écru

Other materials
8-gauge double thread canvas
Refer to the Upholstery & Making Up chapter on page 124 to see how to make a template for your stool and to estimate how much canvas you will need.
Upholstery materials as on page 125 if you wish to cover the footstool yourself.

Working the needlepoint
The chart for the bow part of the design is shown below. Each square of the chart represents one cross stitch. The yarn numbers are given in the colour key.

The four ribbons are made up of elements from the chart given with the Bed Linen with Trailing Ribbons project on pages 68–9. Substitute the tapestry wool colours listed above when following this chart.

7110

7137

7107

7849

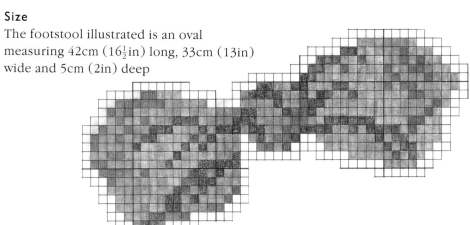

To help with positioning the motifs, refer to the photographs of the footstool. Begin with the double bow. Stitch one bow motif from the chart in cross stitch. Then work another bow motif at right angles to it. Add the ribbons from the bow out to each side. Finally, work the background in tent stitch, inserting red cross stitches at intervals.

Making up the footstool

Stretch the needlepoint back into shape if necessary (see stretching instructions on page 17). Instructions on how to upholster a stool are given in the Upholstery & Making Up chapter on page 124. Alternatively, you may wish to have your stool professionally upholstered.

*t*he bow motif is used twice to form a rosette at the centre of the footstool.

r ibbon cushion with tassels

I chose the glowing colours in this needle-point cushion to reflect the colour combination in the wonderful decorative tassels. Pearl cottons were the perfect choice for the lustrous finish I was seeking.

The ribbons intertwine with one another, shimmering as they loop over the cushion. To add interest, a dragonfly and moth flit by,

reflecting the ribbons' hues. These motifs are taken from page 41 in the Fruit & Butterflies chapter. By placing them on this cushion, I wanted to show how various elements from different projects throughout the book can be combined to make a satisfying finished design which can be tailored to fit your individual requirements.

*l*uxurious pearl cottons make this cushion decorated with fluttering ribbons a very special project. The dragonfly and moth reflect the glorious colours of the ribbons and tassels.

Size
36.5 × 31cm ($14\frac{1}{2}$ × $12\frac{1}{4}$in)

Yarns
DMC coton perlé No. 5
Ribbons, dragonfly and moth
One skein each of the following colours:
Greens (dark to light) 501, 991, 992, 993
Crimsons (dark to light)
3350, 326, 309, 335
Golds (dark to light) 781, 783, 725, 726
Blues (dark to light) 517, 806, 518, 807
Background
13 skeins écru

Other materials
Piece of 18-gauge mono canvas measuring
46.5 × 41cm ($18\frac{1}{2}$ × $16\frac{1}{4}$in)
Piece of backing fabric measuring
40 × 34cm (16 × $13\frac{1}{2}$in)
Tassels to match

Working the needlepoint
The various ribbons are made up of elements from the chart shown on pages 68–9. The charts for the dragonfly and moth designs are on page 41. Each square of the charts represents one tent stitch.

The yarn numbers given in the colour key for the ribbon refer specifically to the colours used for the Bed Linen with Trailing Ribbons project. You will need to substitute the colours listed above when following the charts. Substitute the colours for the dragonfly and moth in the same way. To help with positioning the motifs, refer to page 24 and to the photographs shown here.

Making up the cushion
Stretch the needlepoint back into shape if necessary (see stretching instructions on page 17). Trim the excess canvas to 1.2cm ($\frac{1}{2}$in) for turnings. Cut out a piece of backing fabric and stitch the cushion cover together as shown on page 126, adding a zip if required. Sew tassels to each corner.

animals & alphabets

the splendid stag with his doe, the lithe hare, the robust boar and its young, the brilliant cockerel and the fluffy chick are all traditional in needlepoint and cross stitch, representing the hunt and the homestead. With this selection of motifs you can arrange varied scenes of great character. Animals were often prominent on samplers and, in this chapter, I also include those vital elements of any sampler – the letters of the alphabet and the numerals. Using letters and numbers, you can personalize your work by signing and dating it or by stitching a significant phrase on to a birth or wedding sampler.

these children's chairs are individually designed, but linked by the animal theme to make a pair. With their charm and special appeal, they will become unique family heirlooms.

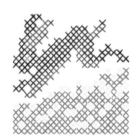

b a b y   b i b s

For a basic project using lettering these little gingham-trimmed bibs are delightfully simple to embroider. Bibs are always a welcome and useful gift for a baby, and personalized ones are all the more appreciated, whether decorated with the baby's name or with a multilingual influence like the ones shown here. The Aida fabric looks fresh and crisp, and is also practical as it washes well. Each bib took only about an hour to stitch, so is ideal for a first attempt at cross stitch.

*t*hese practical baby bibs are useful and easy to stitch. Why not stitch your baby's name to make the bib all the more personal?

Size
Each finished bib measures about 19cm ($7\frac{1}{2}$in) across and 21cm ($8\frac{1}{4}$in) in total length

Yarns
DMC stranded cotton
One skein each of the following colours:
BABY bib
797 blue
BAMBINO bib
307 yellow
BÉBÉ bib
602 pink

Other materials
For each bib illustrated:
Piece of 11 count white Aida fabric measuring 23 × 50cm (9 × 20in)
0.5m ($\frac{5}{8}$yd) blue, yellow or pink gingham, 90cm (36in) wide
0.8m ($\frac{7}{8}$yd) narrow piping cord

Working the cross stitch
Make a paper pattern for the bib shape, adjusting the size according to the age of the baby. Tack the outline of the bib front on to the Aida fabric.

To help with positioning the letters you are going to use, mark the vertical centre of the fabric with a line of tacking thread. Draw your word, or alternatively the baby's name,

on to graph paper and find the centre point. Begin stitching here, so that the letters will be centred on the fabric.

The chart for the letters is shown on page 91. Each square of the chart represents one cross stitch. Work each cross stitch over one block of the fabric, using three strands of stranded cotton in the appropriate colour.

Add a little decorative motif at the beginning and end of the word if you wish.

Making up the bib

Cut out the bib front and back from the Aida fabric, adding 1cm ($\frac{3}{8}$in) turnings all round. Cut out strips of gingham on the bias and make up as piping as shown on page 127, long enough to fit around the edge of the bib with extra gingham (without piping cord) for the ties.

Place the bib front and back right sides together with the piping in between. Stitch around the edge with a 1cm ($\frac{3}{8}$in) turning, leaving a gap all round the neck edge to turn through. Finish off the ties and neck edge.

a nimal place-mats and napkins

Traditional cross stitch animals leap all over these large napkins for children, while, edging the place-mats, the fence border with cockerel or chicks guards the child's plate. These table sets are fun to work and have a rustic charm, perfect for a country setting indoors or outdoors.

Size
Each napkin measures 39cm (15½in) square

Each place-mat measures 45 × 33cm (18 × 13in)

Yarns
DMC stranded cotton
The main colours for each animal are listed below. Toning colours are taken from the other animals.
One skein each of the following colours:
Chick
307 yellow

Cockerel
816 crimson, 451 grey
Boar and baby boar, hare and fence
Browns (dark to light)
3781, 3790. 3045, 3782

Other materials

DMC 12-count chequered evenweave fabric
The fabric requirement for each napkin and place-mat is as its finished size

Working the cross stitch

The charts for the animal and fence designs are shown below and throughout the chapter. Each square of the charts represents one cross stitch. Work each stitch over one block of the fabric, using three strands of stranded cotton. Use the colours specified above, combining them as you wish.

For the napkin, place the motifs at random within the chequered squares. For the place-mat, position the fence border across the top edge, leaving 4cm (1½in) of extra fabric beyond the top of the fence to allow for the fringing.

Making up the place-mat or napkin

When the embroidery is complete, pull out threads to make a 2cm (¾in) fringe around the edge of the mat or napkin. To strengthen the fringed edge, work a line of zigzag machine stitching around the edge first, then fringe up to this line.

*Y*ou can stitch all your favourite farmyard and countryside animals on to these place-mats and napkins. They are finished with a simple fringed edge. The chart for the cockerel (left) can be used for a hen by omitting the tail.

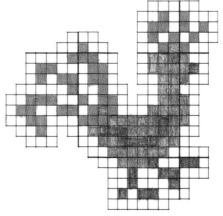

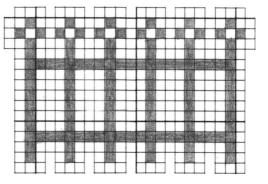

*t*raditional sampler

Samplers were originally used instead of books to record needlework designs and would have been kept folded in the work-basket for constant reference. Many of them were made by very young girls who were expected to practise their stitches at the same time as learning their letters and various moralistic verses.

Abigail is ten and was tempted to design this sampler herself, with a little help. As she was to work accurately, she planned her composition on squared paper beforehand, combining her letters and numbers with a simple arrangement of animals and completing her work in traditional fashion with her name and date of birth. She decided on subdued tones of browns, green and crimson for her threads in sympathy with the beautiful antique samplers she greatly admires at the Victoria and Albert Museum in London.

The fabric she chose for her sampler was a 36-count evenweave linen, which was demanding. However, as she worked, she was inspired by each completed letter to launch herself into the next. In order to facilitate her calculations and act as a constant check, I tacked lengths of thread through the centre folds of her work, with corresponding pink lines through her squared chart.

Size
The completed sampler measures
29×35cm ($11\frac{1}{2} \times 13\frac{3}{4}$in)

Yarns
DMC stranded cotton
One skein each of the following colours:
Letters and numerals
498 crimson
Animals
The main colour for each animal is listed below. Toning colours are taken from the other animals.

Stag
938 dark brown
Doe
640 mid brown
Boar
640 mid brown
Baby boar
3046 honey
Cockerel
3045 dark honey
Chick
3046 honey
Border
890 dark green
498 crimson

Other materials
Piece of 36-count evenweave linen
measuring 44×50cm ($17\frac{1}{2} \times 19\frac{3}{4}$in)

Working the cross stitch
The chart for the capital letters, numerals and border is shown on page 91. The charts for the animals are shown throughout the chapter. Each square of the charts represents one cross stitch.

To help with positioning the motifs, mark the centre of the fabric each way with lines of contrasting tacking thread. Work each cross stitch over two threads of the fabric, using two strands of stranded cotton in the colours specified above or to your own choice.

Find the centre point of each line and begin stitching here, so that the letters will be centred on the fabric. When you come to add your name and the date, work out the arrangement of letters and numbers on graph paper first.

When the sampler is complete, add the border illustrated or one of your choice.

Framing the sampler
For an expert finish, I would recommend having your sampler framed by a professional picture framer.

OPPOSITE
*t*imeless in its appeal, the sampler is a unique personal statement. My daughter, Abigail, worked hard on her creation and is proud of the result.

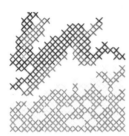

n ursery sampler

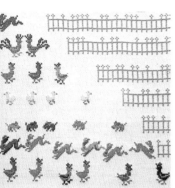

a musingly, my younger daughter, Tiphaine, and I failed to count our hens correctly in spite of much checking when working the sampler project. Nevertheless, many memories of a happy summer are evoked when looking at it.

This combination of animals and numbers as a teaching chart would look charming in any nursery. The simple pattern construction in rows was a relatively straightforward arrangement for Tiphaine, aged eight, to tackle. We chose a 14-count Aida fabric for her, which is easy to work with but still fine enough to look 'grown-up'. I marked out her rows with tacking threads and we designed one row at a time.

I found that Tiphaine's concentration span when working the nursery sampler was about three quarters of an hour. Allowing her to work at her own pace and giving her lots of encouragement were good ploys for her continued enthusiasm for the project.

Size
The completed sampler measures
46 × 47cm (18 × 18½ in) from border edge
to border edge

Yarns
DMC stranded cotton
Numerals and border
Two skeins of 820 dark blue
Fence
Three skeins of 3782 brown
Animals
The main colours for each animal are listed below, but they are combined in different ways to add interest.

One skein each of the following colours:
Chicks
307 yellow
Cockerels
816 crimson, 451 grey
Boars, hens, hares, stag and doe
Browns (dark to light)
3781, 3790, 3045, 3782

Other materials
Piece of 14-count Aida fabric measuring
66 × 67cm (26 × 26½ in)

Working the cross stitch
The charts for the animals and the fence are shown throughout the chapter. Each square of the charts represents one cross stitch. Work each stitch over one block of the fabric, using 3 strands of stranded cotton. Vary the colours in each row of animals as you wish.

To help a child to position the motifs correctly, mark the base of each row with a line of tacking stitches, spacing them 20 blocks apart. Begin working the cross stitch at the top left-hand corner.

Use the photograph opposite to help you with stitching the border, or work a border of your choice, counting the fabric threads to ensure that the corners turn correctly.

Framing the sampler
For an expert finish, I would recommend having your sampler framed by a professional picture framer.

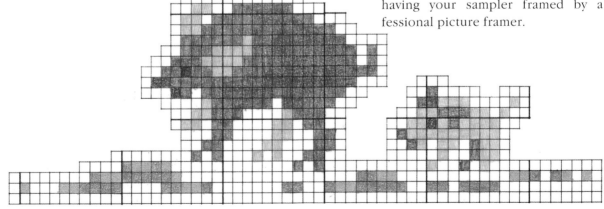

Children's animal chairs

These diminutive chairs are little gems which I found in an antique shop some years ago when my children were much younger. It is interesting to note that, although the two projects *are dissimilar in design, they remain a well-suited pair because I have used the same basic motifs and have chosen harmonizing background colours.*

*d*oes, boars, cockerels, hares and chicks are arranged in straight rows on the crimson chair.

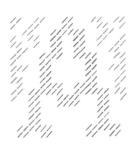

*O*n the green chair, the animals are grouped in a scenic composition, quite different from the geometric arrangement of the crimson chair (opposite).

*t*his close-up of the crimson chair shows the animals walking back and forth in rows, beginning with the largest, the does, at the front, decreasing in size to the smallest chicks.

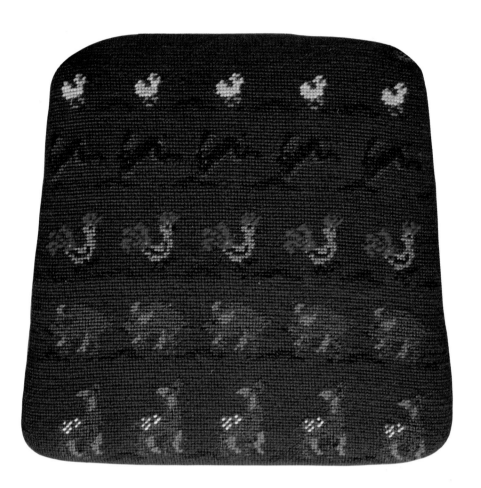

Size
The chairs illustrated measure 34cm (13½in) from front to back, 33cm (13in) wide and 5cm (2in) deep

Yarns
DMC tapestry wool
I have not given yarn quantities for the background colours as this will vary depending on the size of your chair. To estimate how much yarn you might need, refer to page 12.

Project 1: Crimson chair
Crimson background
7110
Green tufts of grass
One skein each of 7329, 7387

Project 2: Green chair
Green background
7389
Red tufts of grass
One skein each of 7198, 7107

Both chairs
The main colours for each animal are listed below, but they are combined in different ways to add interest.
One skein each of the following colours:
Doe
Browns (dark to light)
7499, 7477, 7450, 7515
Stag
Browns (dark to light) 7515, 7499, 7497
Boar
Browns (dark to light) 7515, 7497, 7477

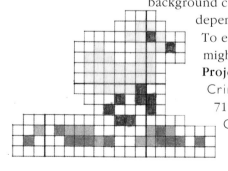

On the green chair, the animals gather in sociable groups. Choosing animals of the forest glade or the farmyard, it is great fun to create your own composition.

Hare
Browns (dark to light) 7515, 7499
Cockerel
Red 7849, grey 7275, brown 7515
Chick
Yellow 7725, browns 7497, 7477

Other materials
For each chair
10-gauge double thread canvas
Refer to the Upholstery & Making Up chapter on page 124 to see how to make a template for your chair and to estimate how much canvas you will need.
Upholstery materials as on page 125 if you wish to cover a drop-in chair seat yourself.

Working the needlepoint
The charts for the animals and the tufts of grass are shown below and throughout the chapter. Each square of the charts represents one tent stitch. Use the colours specified above for the animals, combining them as you wish.

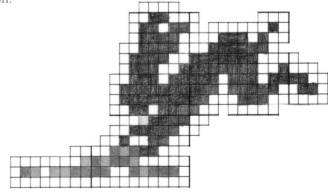

Project 1: Crimson chair

Calculate how many rows of animals you will need to make a regular, evenly spaced design on your chair. Beginning at one corner, stitch the animals to and fro across the canvas with the tufts of grass beneath them. When the animals are complete, fill in the background colour.

Project 2: Green chair

Decide how you wish to arrange the animals into groups, remembering that some will be placed behind others so you need to follow only part of the appropriate chart here. Incorporate tufts of grass into the overall composition.

To help you with planning the design, refer to page 24 and to the photograph shown on the previous page. If you find it useful, draw your design on to plain paper or plan it on graph paper first. Begin by stitching the groups of animals and then fill in the background colour.

Making up the chairs

Stretch the needlepoint back into shape if necessary (see stretching instructions on page 17). Instructions on how to upholster a simple drop-in chair seat are given in the Upholstery & Making Up chapter on page 124, but you may wish to have a more complex chair professionally upholstered.

*t*he stag and his doe are featured as a pair on the Traditional Sampler on page 82, the Nursery Sampler on page 85 and the green Animal Chair on page 87.

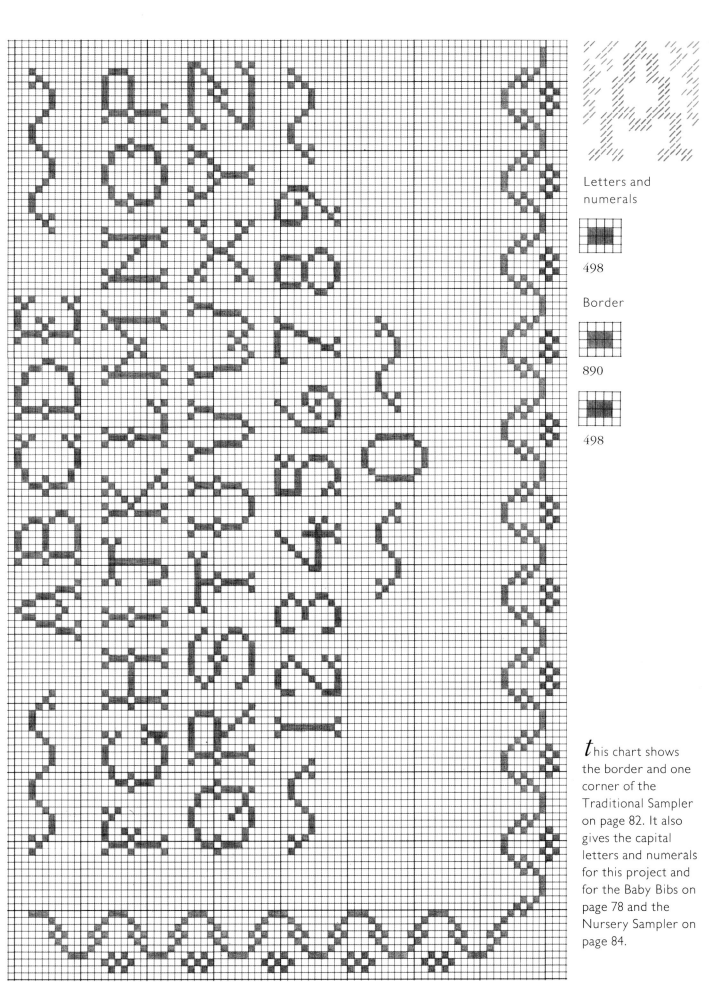

Letters and numerals

498

Border

890

498

*t*his chart shows the border and one corner of the Traditional Sampler on page 82. It also gives the capital letters and numerals for this project and for the Baby Bibs on page 78 and the Nursery Sampler on page 84.

leaves & berries

leaves are very versatile to use in embroidery and always look fresh and welcoming. In this chapter I have arranged leaves into garlands and as trailing designs, as well as combining them with berries of different kinds. Berries are delightful motifs which are colourful, quick and easy to embroider and perfect to combine with other patterns. I have used a variety of berries – strawberries, blackberries, redcurrants and holly berries – arranging them in groups on jam jar covers, singly on a child's dress, in a row along the bib of an apron or tucked among the leaves of a festive wreath.

*b*erry designs not only look charming on these jam jar covers, but provide a decorative way of labelling the contents.

Chef's apron with berries

Ripe luscious berries, which I love to gather from the hedgerows or from the garden, translate beautifully into embroidery motifs and add a splash of colour wherever they are used. The redcurrants and blackberries on this starched white apron for my kitchen will keep my autumnal harvesting with me throughout the year. They make a beautiful design which could also be used very successfully on table linen. I have stitched the berries on to the apron bib over waste canvas, as the threads of the fabric cannot be counted as they can with evenweave fabric.

Berries are a very versatile motif. Just change the colour and you can have blackcurrants and raspberries on the apron instead. Or, for a festive look, change the redcurrants to white mistletoe berries and red holly berries.

Size
27cm (10½in) across bib front

Yarns
DMC stranded cotton
Approximately one skein each of the following colours:

Blackberries
823 dark blue, 902 maroon, 498 red
Redcurrants
Reds (dark to light) 902, 816, 498
Dark blue 823
Leaves
Greens (dark to light) 890, 936, 987

Other materials
White cotton apron
Piece of 11-gauge waste canvas measuring
33 × 14cm (13 × 5½in)

Working the cross stitch
The charts for the berry designs are shown below and overleaf. Each square of the charts represents one cross stitch.

Tack the waste canvas to the apron bib and embroider the berries with three strands of stranded cotton. The yarn numbers are given in the colour key. Position the blackberries to the left of the redcurrants, referring to the photographs shown here to help you. When the motifs are complete, remove the waste canvas as described on page 16.

*t*his chart shows the redcurrant design.

Redcurrants

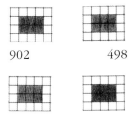

902   498

816   823

Leaves

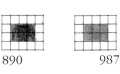

890   987

936

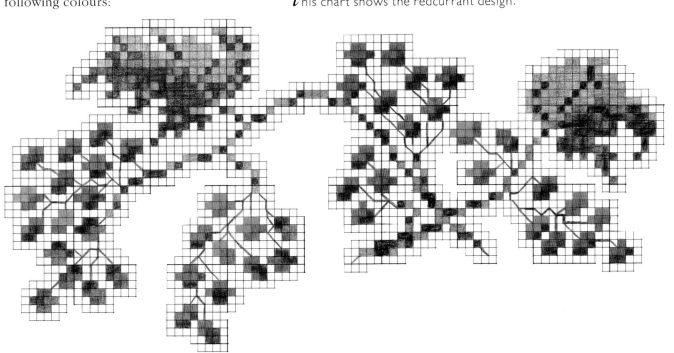

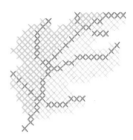

a detail of the berry design illustrates how the blackberry sprig joins the redcurrants. The chart for the blackberries is shown below.

Blackberries

823

902

498

Leaves

890

936

987

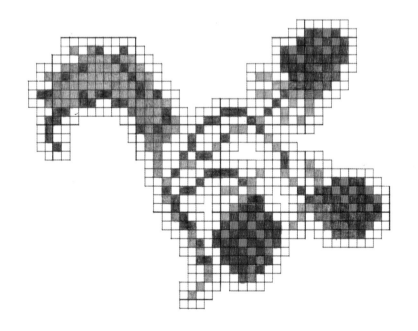

a country kitchen with embroidered accessories looks warm and welcoming. The cross stitch berries would also look luscious on a tablecloth, napkins or tea towels.

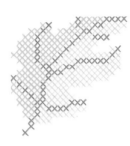

j am jar covers

On my first trip to Spain at the age of twelve, I remember being impressed with the delicate muslin caps, weighted down with beads, which covered the tall glass pitchers of freshly squeezed orange juice in the cafés. The attractive appearance of these covers inspired me to embellish some jam jars in a similar way, using embroidery instead of beads for my decorative effect.

I have used strawberries, blackberries and redcurrants for my motifs, which have the added advantage of labelling the jams. The covers are finished with a machine zigzag edging and are tied on with ribbon.

Size
20cm (8in) in diameter

Yarns
DMC stranded cotton
For each jam jar cover, one skein each of the following colours:
Blackberries
823 dark blue, 902 maroon, 498 dark red
Redcurrants
Reds (dark to light) 902, 816, 498
Blackberry and redcurrant stems
Greens (dark to light) 936, 987
Strawberries
816 crimson, 321 scarlet, 676 gold,
677 light gold
Strawberry leaves
Greens (dark to light) 319, 469

Other materials
For each jam jar cover:
Piece of 25-count white evenweave fabric measuring 25cm (10in) square
Ribbon to match
Sewing thread to match

Working the cross stitch
The berry designs are taken from the charts on pages 95, 96 and 101. Each square of the charts represents one cross stitch. Work each cross stitch over two threads of the evenweave fabric, using three strands of stranded cotton. The yarn numbers are given in the colour key. Position the berries centrally on the fabric or around the edge as shown in the photograph.

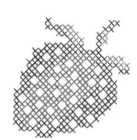

Making up the jam jar covers

Mark a circle 20cm (8in) in diameter (or to suit your jam jar) around the motif on the fabric. Work close machine zigzag stitch around the circle, then cut away the excess fabric as close as possible to the stitching.

Alternatively, you could turn under a narrow hem all round the cover and then trim the edge with colourful rickrack braid or white lace. You could even add loops of small glass beads to weight down the covers in traditional fashion.

*b*eautifully decorated jam jars, tied up with crisp bows, are delightful to present as a gift.

*C*hild's strawberry dress

*U*sing the waste canvas method, fruit motifs can be stitched on to any background.

Strawberry

816

321   Leaves

 676   319

 677   469

White and full, this child's dress is rather special. The cross stitch strawberries on the cuffs and sash look fresh enough to pick and personalize the outfit in a charming way. They are quick and simple to work over waste canvas. I made this dress myself, but you could use the idea with any dress of a similar style, buying wide ribbons for the sash and adding a ready-made white collar if you wish. By using waste canvas, small motifs like the strawberry can be worked on all kinds of children's and adults' garments and fashion accessories.

Yarns
DMC stranded cotton
One skein each of the following colours:
Strawberries
816 crimson, 321 scarlet, 676 gold,
677 light gold
Leaves
Greens (dark to light) 319, 469

Other materials
12-gauge waste canvas
Wide ribbon for sash

Working the cross stitch
The charts for the strawberry designs are shown on this page. Each square of the charts represents one cross stitch.

Decide where you wish to position each strawberry motif and tack a piece of waste canvas measuring about 5cm (2in) square at this point. For a double motif, increase this measurement to 7×5cm ($2\frac{3}{4} \times 2$in). (If you are sewing the dress yourself, it is best to embroider the motif on to the cuffs before making them up.) Work the cross stitch over the waste canvas, using three strands of stranded cotton. The yarn numbers are given in the colour key.

When the strawberry motifs are complete, remove the waste canvas strand by strand as described on page 16.

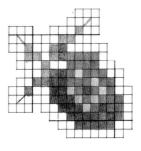

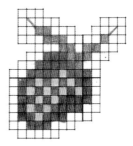

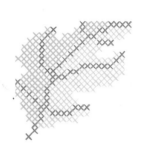

*f*rilled cushion with leaf garland

*a*s a chair is frequently hidden from sight beneath the table, the ties on this cushion deserve particular attention.

Grasses and leaves are entwined into a summer garland on this cushion to tie on to a wooden chair. The design would look equally at home in the kitchen, the dining room or the garden, and the colours of the leaves can be changed to suit all seasons of the year.

The garland is made up of a curve of leaves repeated twice, with a few additional leaves to make up the full circle. This can be adapted to form a border design instead by simply reversing the direction of the curve each time to form an undulating row of intertwined leaves.

I worked the cross stitch directly on to the striped linen fabric, as it was reasonably loosely woven and I was able to fit each cross stitch across the width of a stripe. I like to work on different materials and it is not really necessary to use waste canvas if you feel that you can position the crosses accurately without it.

The cushion has a traditional Scandinavian feel, softened with the gathered frill around the bottom, and is attached to the chair with ties. Most of the time a chair is tucked beneath the table, so it is a good idea to make the most of the ties, which you can still see. As I adore ribbons and ties, I have used them here as both a practical and a decorative feature, repeating some of the leaves from the garland on them.

Size

The cushion illustrated measures 38cm (15in) wide, 35cm (14in) from front to back and 4cm (1½in) deep
The frill is 10cm (4in) deep
Each tie measures 96 × 6cm (38 × 2¼in)

Yarns

DMC stranded cotton
One skein each of the following colours:
Greens (dark to light) 890, 987, 470, 471, 472
Browns (dark to light) 3781, 3045

Other materials

For the cushion illustrated, you will need:
1m (1⅛yd) striped upholstery fabric, 140cm (54in) wide. The fabric illustrated has 10 stripes to 2.5cm (1in)
0.7m (¾yd) lining fabric, 140cm (54in) wide
Thick polyester wadding for filling
Dressmaker's carbon paper

Working the cross stitch

The chart for the garland design and the leaves for the ties are shown overleaf. The curve of leaves is repeated twice, once as a mirror image, to form most of the circle, and an additional sprig of leaves is added at the bottom right-hand corner of the cushion to complete the shape.

Each square of the chart represents one cross stitch. On the cushion illustrated, each cross stitch is worked over one stripe of the fabric, using three strands of stranded cotton. The yarn numbers are given in the colour key. The chart shows some of the leaves in brown as an alternative colourway.

Positioning the motifs

Refer to the photographs of the cushion to see how to assemble the various elements of the design. The method of working the embroidery involves two different techniques. For the first section of the garland, you follow the chart. For the second section, you mark the design on to the fabric and fill it in without following the chart.

Begin stitching the curve of leaves at the bottom left-hand corner, following the chart. When this is complete, place tracing paper over the embroidery and mark the outline. Turn over the tracing paper and transfer the outline as a mirror image to the top right-hand part of the cushion, using dressmaker's carbon paper.

Then fill in the outline with cross stitch, echoing the colours of the leaves you have

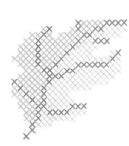

*t*he close-up view of the striped cushion shows how the elements of the design are linked together. Make the curve of leaves shown in the chart (below) work for you, whether you use it on its own or combine two curves to form a wreath shape.

already worked. Finally, stitch the extra sprig of leaves to complete the circle.

If you prefer, you could work the second curve of leaves as a mirror image directly from the chart. However, it will then be at a slightly different angle and will need to be moved further around the circle. Fill in the gap with a few extra leaves.

Work a few overlapping leaves at the end of one or both of the ties.

Making up the cushion

Trim the fabric to fit the shape of your chair seat if necessary, adding 4cm (1½in) all round for the depth and 1.5cm (⅝in) extra all round for turnings. Cut out the cushion lining to fit the shape of the chair seat plus turnings. Cut out a length of fabric and lining plus turnings for each tie. For the frill, measure around three sides of the cushion and make up a gathered frill to fit.

Stitch a dart at each corner of the cushion. Stitch on the frill around three sides, right sides facing. You could also add a shorter frill at the back if you wish.

Attach the ties at the back corners. Insert the wadding, fold in the turnings of the lining and slipstitch the lining to the base of the cushion.

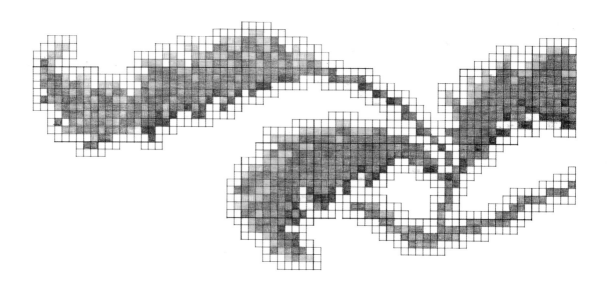

890

987

470

471

472

3781

3045

W reath and berries cushion

Wreaths always look sumptuous and are wonderful to design and stitch. I have given this needlepoint wreath its distinctive character by combining the two main elements in this chapter – the garland of leaves and grasses, and the berries. I have set them against a dark charcoal background to throw the rich colours into relief. The trailing foliage represents all the seasons of the year to me: the grasses conjure up springtime, the green leaves suggest the lushness of summer, the red leaves remind me of autumn and the berries of winter.

The formation of the wreath is quite simple. One curve of trailing leaves is a direct image of the other and, by moving these main motifs apart a little, I achieved an oval. I filled in the extra space by repeating a sprig of red leaves combined with a few berries in one place and by inserting berries and their leaves in the other. To add interest to an otherwise large plain area of background, I took a single berry motif and repeated it within the wreath to form a regular pattern.

Size
An oval measuring 56cm (22in) long and 50cm (19¾in) wide

Yarns
DMC tapestry wool
Leaves, grasses and berries
Reds
Three skeins each of 7110, 7108
One skein each of 7147, 7137
Greens
Four skeins of 7387
Three skeins of 7379
Two skeins each of 7346, 7768
One skein of 7429
Blue
One skein of 7823
Background
40 skeins of charcoal 7624

Other materials
Piece of 10-gauge mono canvas measuring 66 × 60cm (26 × 23¾in)
Piece of backing fabric measuring 58.5 × 52.5cm (23 × 20¾in)
1.8m (2yd) twisted cord
1.8m (2yd) fringing
Cushion pad to fit

Working the needlepoint
The chart for the wreath design is shown on pages 104–5 and for the berries on page 95. Each square of the charts represents one tent stitch. The yarn numbers given in the colour keys refer to different projects, so you will need to substitute the colours listed above when following the charts.

The curve of leaves is repeated twice, one opposite the other, to form the basic oval arrangement. The spaces are filled in with additional sprigs of leaves and clusters of berries taken from the two charts. To help with positioning the motifs, refer to the photograph shown here or work out your own arrangement.

When you have completed the wreath, work the berries over the background area. Then fill in the background itself.

Making up the cushion
Stretch the needlepoint back into shape if necessary (see stretching instructions on page 17). Trim the excess canvas to 1.2cm (½in) for turnings. Cut out the backing fabric to match. Make up the cushion with a trimming of fringing and twisted cord as on pages 126–7, inserting the fringing when you are stitching on the backing fabric and sewing on the twisted cord when the cushion cover is turned through to the right side.

a demanding but delightful needlepoint project, this wreath design combines leaves and grasses with a berry motif. The charcoal background sets off the warm colours.

plaids
& thistles

*P*laid, or tartan, is a traditional *Scottish pattern which has charmed generations and has travelled worldwide. When using plaid designs in needlepoint or cross stitch, you will be fascinated by the learning experience of combining the colours. As the bands of colour cross one another, you have to create a new area of colour. For example, as blue crosses grey, you need to use a bluish-grey yarn at the intersection. This subtle blending of tones means that plaids fit into any interior, traditional or modern. The thistle is the perfect partner for a plaid design, used singly or in a posy, and also looks pretty on a plain background.*

*P*laid and thistle designs complement each other perfectly, whether you use traditional colours or experiment with an imaginative palette of your own.

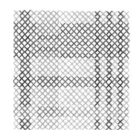

t ablecloth with plaid border

Bands of plaid in reds, blues and greys create a dramatic border on this pink tablecloth. By using an unusual colour combination on a pastel background, a familiar pattern looks intriguingly different. The lines of plaid are worked in cross stitch and subtly change colour wherever they cross one another. The background fabric shows through to become an integral part of the design.

Size
The cloth illustrated measures approximately 106cm (41¾in) square

*p*laids are always fascinating to work. This pattern forms a vibrant border on a tablecloth.

Yarns
DMC stranded cotton
4 skeins each of the following colours:
Reds (dark to light) 902, 815, 816
Blues (dark to light) 823, 311, 820
Greys (dark to light) 451, 452
Pink 602
Purple 550

Other materials
Piece of pink 11-count Aida fabric measuring 110cm (43in) square

Working the cross stitch
The chart for the bands of plaid is shown opposite. Each square of the chart represents one cross stitch. Work each cross stitch over one block of fabric, using three strands of stranded cotton. The yarn numbers are given in the colour key.

Begin with the corner motif, positioning it 7cm (2¾in) from each edge of the fabric. Then continue with the bands of plaid. The

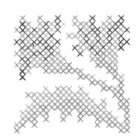

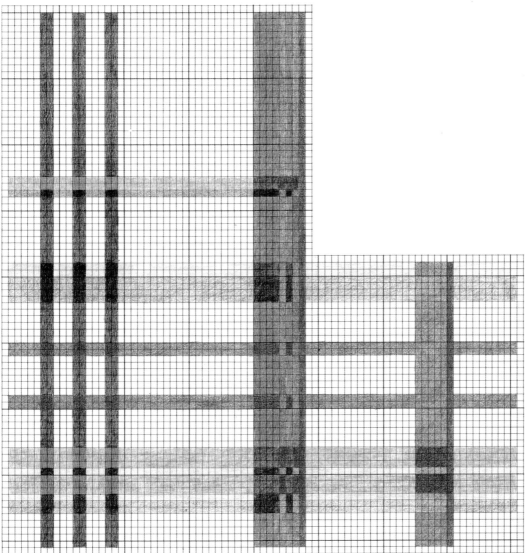

902

815

816

823

311

820

451

452

602

550

chart shows one pattern repeat for each band. Work the appropriate repeat pattern five times along each side, then add the other corners, checking that they are working out correctly.

If you wish to make a tablecloth that is a different size from the one illustrated, your border will probably end at a different part of the plaid pattern. In this case, choose an appropriate combination of lines to finish with, so that you can continue these around the corner as your next border. Various borders can be created from this design, so have fun experimenting with a few. You will have to count out the number of squares in the pattern repeats and the threads of the fabric if you want to be really accurate with the positioning.

Making up the tablecloth
Turn up a 1cm ($\frac{3}{8}$in) double hem all round the tablecloth, mitring the corners.

*p*astel plaid footstool

This chunky little footstool, smartly covered in plaid with a modern emphasis, is quick and easy to complete using an eight-gauge canvas. Having a regular pattern, it is an ideal project for the beginner, and the frequent changes of colour make it stimulating to work.

The stool itself has a very simple construction. Some bought legs are attached to a plywood base with a thick layer of foam rubber on top. Upholstery details for a basic stool are given on page 125, so you can do the covering yourself to make this a more economical project.

Size

The stool illustrated is 44cm (17½in) long, 34 .m (13½in) wide and 7cm (2¾in) deep

Yarns

I have not given yarn quantities here as this will vary depending on the size of your stool. To estimate how much yarn you might need, refer to page 12.
DMC tapestry wool (listed from dark to light):
Bands of plaid
Crimsons 7110, 7137
Pinks 7600, 7603
Greys 7275, 7273, 7282
Purples 7247, 7245
Dark blues 7308, 7823, 7820
Slate blues 7297, 7591
Background
Fawns 7520, 7450, 7500
Pale pinks 7853, 7121, 7191
Pinky beiges 7200, 7451, 7170

Other materials

8-gauge double thread canvas
Refer to the Upholstery & Making Up chapter on page 124 to see how to make a template for your stool and to estimate how much canvas you will need. For the size of stool illustrated, you will need a piece of canvas measuring 78 × 68cm (30½ × 27in).
Upholstery materials as on page 125 if you wish to cover the stool yourself.

Working the needlepoint

The chart for the plaid design is shown on page 123. Each square of the chart represents one tent stitch. One pattern repeat is shown on the chart. The yarn numbers are given in the colour key.

Decide which part of the design you would like to centre on the stool. I have made a feature of the two bold widthways bands in blue/purple and bright pink. Find the centre of the canvas and count out where to start stitching the first repeat pattern so that your chosen bands will be positioned correctly to make a balanced composition.

Making up the stool

Stretch the needlepoint back into shape if necessary (see stretching instructions on page 17). Instructions on how to upholster a stool are given in the Upholstery & Making Up chapter on page 124. Alternatively, you may wish to have your stool upholstered professionally.

a detail of the needlepoint plaid pattern shows the subtle colour changes where the different bands cross one another.

p laid rug with thistles

Thistle sprigs are scattered across the corner of this richly coloured travelling rug, which would look wonderful draped across the back of a chair or sofa, but is practical enough to use in the car or at the end of a bed. The thistle motifs are worked in cross stitch over waste canvas, and are easy to place by using the plaid squares as a guide. The soft fabric of the rug is a delight to work with and the stranded cottons I used for the embroidery blend beautifully with the wool, with an interesting contrast of shiny and matt textures.

Size
The small thistle motifs are about 10cm (4in) high and the larger ones about 15cm (6in) high

*t*he thistle motif can be worked singly or in sprigs, with leaves or without. Scatter the flowers at random or organize them into a more regular pattern if you wish.

Yarns
DMC stranded cotton
One skein each of the following colours:
Flowers
Blues (dark to light) 311, 820, 792
Purples (dark to light) 550, 552, 553
Leaves and stems
Greens (dark to light) 500, 3362, 522

Other materials
Woollen travelling rug or shawl
11/12-gauge waste canvas

Working the cross stitch
The thistle motifs are taken from the charts shown below and on page 121. Each square of the charts represents one cross stitch.

Decide where you want to place each thistle and tack to the rug a piece of waste canvas measuring 15 × 10cm (6 × 4in) for a small thistle sprig and 20 × 17cm (8 × 6¾in) for a thistle with leaves.

Work the cross stitch over the waste canvas, using three strands of stranded cotton. Use purples or blues for the flowers. When the embroidery is complete, remove the waste canvas as described on page 16.

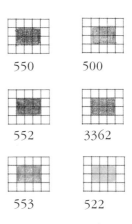

550   500

552   3362

553   522

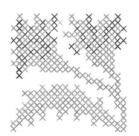

t h i s t l e   w a i s t c o a t

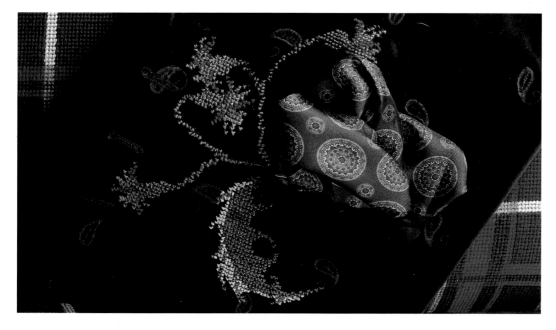

*t*histles tucked into the pocket of a velvet waistcoat add an element of fun to a traditional garment for a man.

In earlier times, men's waistcoats were often embroidered by their loved ones, and there are some exquisite examples of these decorative garments in museums. When I was choosing this waistcoat, I felt that the paisley motif on the velvet would provide an interesting background to the embroidery. Unpicking the lining, I placed my waste canvas so that the thistles would look as though they were tucked into the pocket.

This project was delightfully easy to stitch and, once decorated with the thistles, the waistcoat became more festive and reminded me of a wonderful summer spent in the Highlands of Scotland. Try experimenting on different fabrics and on various garments. A well-placed motif in silky stranded cotton can give a plain garment a unique personal touch.

Size

The thistles measure about 10cm (4in) high and the leaf is about 9cm (3½in) long

Yarns

DMC stranded cotton

One skein each of the following colours:
Flowers
Blues (dark to light) 820, 797, 792
Leaves and stems
Greens (dark to light) 319, 935, 522

Other materials

Piece of 11-gauge waste canvas measuring 20 × 23cm (8 × 9in)
Velvet waistcoat

Working the cross stitch

The chart for the thistles and leaves design is shown on page 121. The thistles on the waistcoat are taken from this grouping, with the stems worked at random. Each square of the chart represents one cross stitch.

Unpick the lining of the waistcoat and tack the piece of waste canvas to the pocket area. Work the cross stitch over the waste canvas, using three strands of stranded cotton in the colours listed above or to your choice. When the embroidery is complete, remove the waste canvas from the motifs as described on page 16. Then re-stitch the lining to the waistcoat.

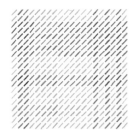

dark plaid stool with thistles

This richly coloured plaid was inspired by the Hunting MacRae tartan, a traditional Scottish pattern. I fell in love with the combination of deep blues and forest greens with crimson, and was intrigued by the way the fine black line running through the design changes subtly as it weaves through the surrounding crimsons, blues, greens and white. The central group of thistles is surrounded by the buckled belt – a traditional Scottish motif.

The more complex plaids are demanding to work, but the intensity and harmony of the rich coloration gave me intense pleasure. After stitching the first pattern repeat, I could continue the plaid without a chart and the design was much admired as I worked on it while travelling by plane or on the train.

Size

The stool illustrated measures 51cm (20in) long, 29cm (11½in) wide and 9cm (3½in) deep

Yarns

I have not given yarn quantities here as this will vary depending on the size of your stool. To estimate how much yarn you might need, refer to page 12.

DMC tapestry wool (listed from dark to light):

Bands of plaid
Blues 7299, 7823, 7796, 7690, 7323
Crimsons and pinks 7147, 7138, 7108, 7107, 7194, 7460
Greens 7429, 7329, 7387, 7406, 7404

Thistle flowers
Blues 7823, 7796

Thistle leaves and stems
Greens 7429, 7329, 7427

Belt
Browns 7801, 7432, 7840

Black

Background to thistles
Mid green 7406

*t*his vibrant plaid attracted a lot of attention while I was working it. Combining the pattern with the thistle and belt motif adds interest to the design.

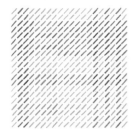

Other materials

10-gauge mono canvas
Refer to the Upholstery & Making Up chapter on page 124 to see how to make a template for your stool and to estimate how much canvas you will need.
Upholstery materials as on page 125 if you wish to cover your stool yourself.

Working the needlepoint

The thistle and belt motif and the plaid design are shown on the charts opposite and on page 122. Each square of the charts represents one tent stitch. One pattern repeat is shown on the chart for the plaid. The yarn numbers are given in the colour key with each chart.

*t*he traditional Scottish thistle and belt motif is the focal point of the stool design.

Work the thistle and belt motif first, beginning at the centre. Then work the plaid design, beginning centrally and working the repeat pattern out to the edges.

Making up the stool

Stretch the needlepoint back into shape if necessary (see stretching instructions on page 17). Instructions on how to upholster a stool are given in the Upholstery & Making Up chapter on page 124. Alternatively, you may wish to have your stool upholstered professionally.

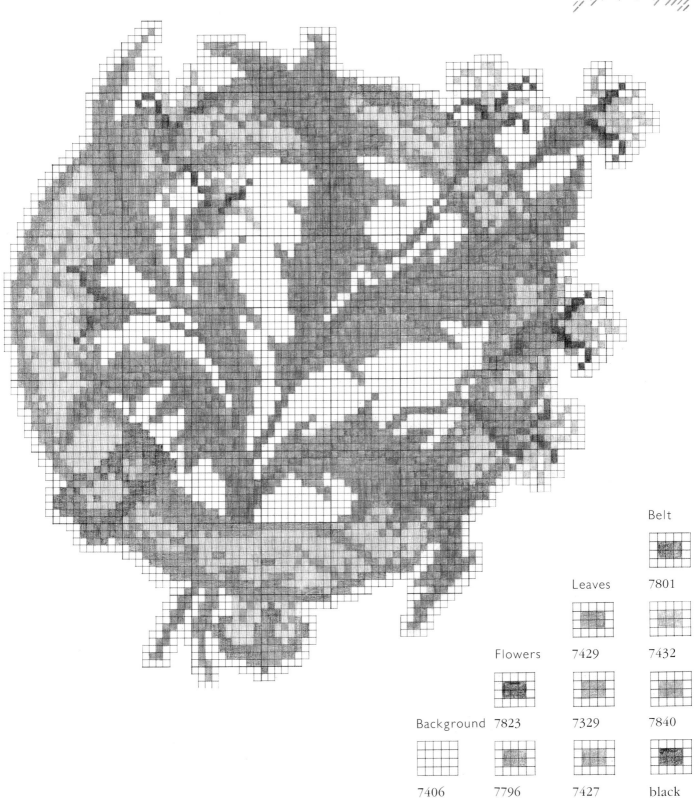

Belt

Leaves   7801

Flowers   7429   7432

Background   7823   7329   7840

7406   7796   7427   black

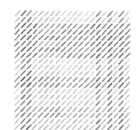

dark plaid stool with thistles

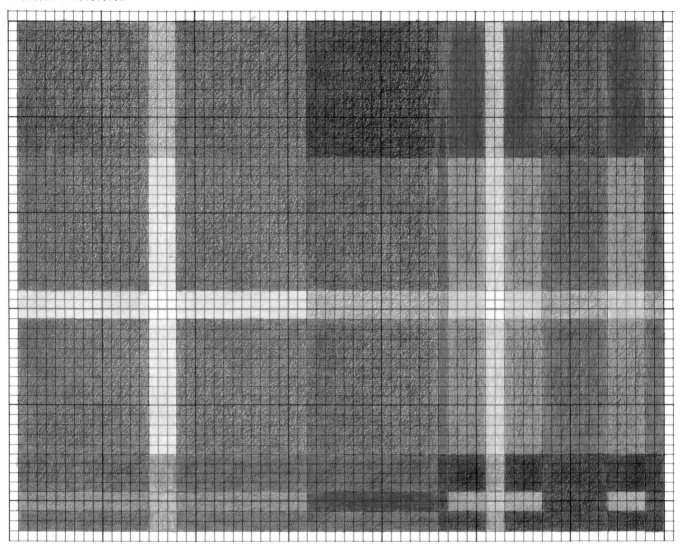

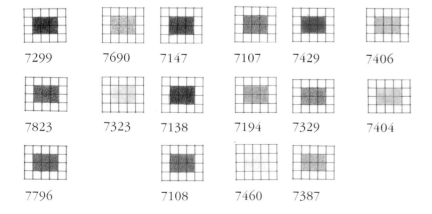

7299	7690	7147	7107	7429	7406
7823	7323	7138	7194	7329	7404
7796		7108	7460	7387	

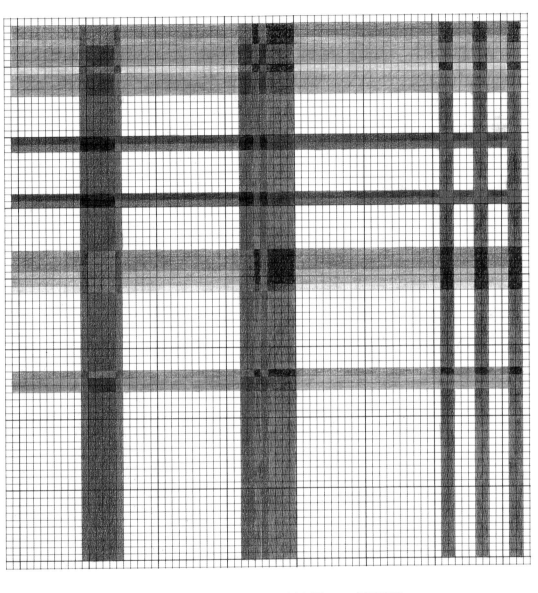

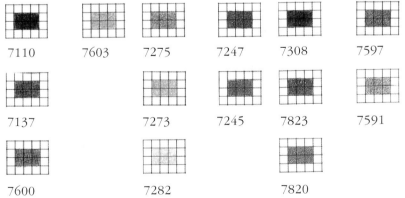

7110	7603	7275	7247	7308	7597

7137	7273	7245	7823	7591

7600	7282	7820

$\mathcal{U}$ pholstery & making up

One of the most attractive ways of using needlepoint is to cover a stool or chair, as it gives a hard-wearing finish which is very suitable for upholstery and can be designed to blend in with your furnishings. In this chapter I explain how to make a template to match the shape of a particular piece of furniture so that you can plan your design and cut out your canvas accordingly. I also show you how you can make a project more economical by upholstering simple pieces such as a footstool yourself. Finally, there are tips for making up cushions.

Making a template

When you are planning a piece of needlepoint to cover a stool or chair, you will need to work out how much canvas to buy. I recommend using old sheeting to help you determine the shape of the templates.

Pin the sheeting all around the seat of the chair or stool, cutting it if necessary to accommodate the chair back or to fit the legs better. Then take a felt tip pen and mark around the edge of the sheeting, where the braid will be. Cut away any excess fabric.

For an upholstered chair back, pin sheeting to this area too. Mark this outline with a felt tip pen in a different colour. Finally, mark the elbow rests, if any.

It is very important to mark all the parts that show, as these are the areas on which you will be designing and stitching. Indicate the back and front or top and bottom of each template too, as they can be rather an odd shape when taken off a chair.

Calculating canvas requirements

Now you can calculate the area of canvas required to cover your furniture. You will need a generous margin all around the edge of the template as, when upholstering, you will need to grasp the excess canvas in order to pull the needlepoint taut over the chair or stool. I find that 10cm (4in) all round is adequate for this. Pin the template to the canvas and mark around the stitching area and outer perimeter with an indelible pen.

Simple upholstery

The following instructions apply to a simple footstool with a solid base or a drop-in chair seat. An economical way of making your own footstool is to use a piece of plywood for the base, with bought wooden legs screwed to the underside. The Pastel Plaid Footstool on page 112 is made in this way.

Materials

Newspaper for making the pattern
Tape measure
Felt tip pen
5cm (2in) thick foam rubber
Multi-purpose glue
Calico
1cm ($\frac{3}{8}$in) thick wadding
Completed needlepoint
Felt for backing
Scissors
Serrated kitchen knife
Staple gun
Decorative braid
Piece of plywood cut to size, and wooden stool legs (if making your own stool)

Measuring the pattern pieces

Place the stool base or drop-in chair base on to a sheet of newspaper and draw around it. Cut out and mark this pattern piece **A**.

Lay pattern piece A on to another sheet of newspaper. Add 10cm (4in) all around. Cut out and mark this pattern piece **B**.

Pattern piece **A** gives you the measurements for cutting out the foam and the felt backing. If you measure all around the outer edges and add a small amount of overlap, you will also have the length for the braid.

Pattern piece **B** gives you the required measurements for the wadding, the calico

and the canvas.

Place pattern piece **A** on to the foam rubber and draw around it with a felt tip pen. Saw the foam to the correct size using the serrated kitchen knife – the sawing motion will ensure a straight cut. Using a multipurpose glue, stick the foam to the base of the stool or chair seat.

Place the calico and the wadding together and pin on pattern piece **B**. Cut out. Do the same with the canvas.

Place the wadding and the calico over the foam attached to the base, ensuring that they are positioned centrally. Fold the edges under the stool or chair base and use the staple gun to staple down one side, enclosing the foam. Repeat this on the remaining sides neatly folding the corners.

Carefully place the completed needle-point centrally over the calico, ensuring that the design is aligned correctly. Staple the canvas into position. Trim the excess material from the underside of the base. Cut out a piece of felt, using pattern piece **A**. Apply multi-purpose glue to the felt and stick in position, covering the raw edges.

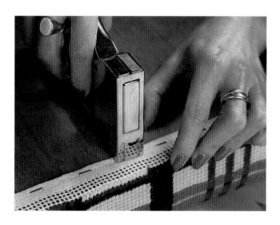

These steps complete the process for upholstering a drop-in chair base or a stool with legs. For a plywood stool base, attach the painted or varnished legs before sticking on the felt.

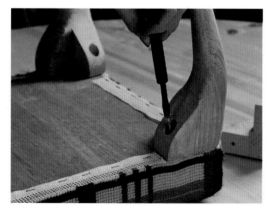

Apply a little multi-purpose glue around the circumference of the stool and attach the braid or fringing as required. Secure the overlap with a staple.

Making up a cushion with a zip

A neat way of inserting a zip into an embroidered cushion cover is to place it centrally on the backing fabric. When you are cutting out the backing fabric to match the front of the cover, add 5cm (2in) to the width for a vertical zip seam.

Fold the fabric in half from side to side and cut along the crease. Stitch each end of the seam up to the zip opening, taking 2.5cm (1in) turnings. Insert the zip into the opening and stitch in place. Leave it slightly open so that you can turn the cushion cover through the opening.

Pin and tack the back of the cushion cover to the front, right sides together. Machine or backstitch around the edge. Clip diagonally across the corners, then turn the cover through to the right side through the zip opening. Insert the cushion pad.

Making up a piped cushion

You can make your own piping to match a cushion by covering piping cord with strips of fabric cut on the bias. To calculate the width of the strips, add the circumference of the piping cord to twice the seam allowance.

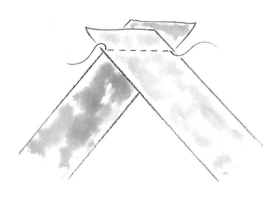

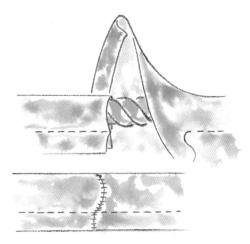

Join bias strips right sides together as shown until you have the length you require. Insert the piping cord, then pin and stitch closed with a zipper foot.

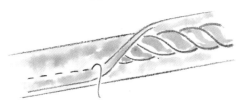

Pin and stitch the piping in place along the seamline of the front of the cushion cover with raw edges aligned. Snip into the corners as shown.

To join the piping neatly where the ends meet, unpick the bias strips a little way and fold the fabric back. Twist the ends of the cord together, then overlap the ends of the bias strips and stitch closed.

Pin and machine or backstitch the cushion back to the cushion front, right sides together, just inside the previous stitching line. Leave an opening to turn the cover through if you have not put in a zip at the back.

Turn the cushion cover through to the right side, insert the cushion pad and sew up the opening by hand.

Trimming a cushion with twisted cord

Twisted cord is an attractive trimming for a needlepoint or cross stitch cushion. Sew it on by hand after turning the cover through to the right side. To prevent the ends of the cord from fraying while you are stitching it on, wrap them with adhesive tape.

Begin stitching at a small opening in the seam allowance at the bottom of the cushion cover and, when the cord is attached, tuck the ends into the gap and stitch up securely.

index